Sebastian Beckmann
Bill Lowenburg
Carina Welsch

ENGLISCH-KRIMI

Spannende Fälle lösen und Englisch lernen

Klasse 7/8

Cornelsen

Die Autoren:

Sebastian Beckmann hat Anglistik, Politische Wissenschaft und Mathematik an der Universität Heidelberg studiert. Seit dem Ende des Referendariats arbeit er an einem Gymnasium in Speyer und forschte zwischenzeitlich mit einem Stipendium der Friedrich-Ebert-Stiftung an der Schnittstelle Literaturwissenschaft/Literaturdidaktik.

Bill Lowenburg hat an der Wilkes University in Pennsylvania Creative Writing studiert und einen Masterabschluss in Bildungs- und Bibliothekswissenschaften. Er unterrichtete 37 Jahre lang an High Schools und Universitäten in den Vereinigten Staaten. Bill Lowenburg ist Autor eines Jugendromans und eines Fotobandes. Momentan arbeitet er an seinem zweiten Roman.

Carina Welsch studierte Anglistik, Amerikanistik und Anglophone Kulturen sowie Geschichtswissenschaften an der Universität des Saarlandes. Nach Lehrtätigkeiten an einer Privatschule in Großbritannien und Beendigung des Referendariats arbeitet sie an einem rheinland-pfälzischen Gymnasium.

Projektleitung: Juliane Maaß, Berlin
Redaktion: Louisa Pabst-Orzechowski, Glienicke/Nordbahn
Umschlaggestaltung: Corinna Babylon, Berlin; Jule Kienecker, Berlin
Umschlagillustrationen: shutterstock/Sonya illustration (Fingerabdruck); shutterstock/Tobias Steinert (Hintergrund)
Innenteil: shutterstock/Sonya illustration (Detektivmütze, Fingerabdruck und Lupe);
shutterstock/Tobias Steinert (Hintergrund)
Illustrationen: Dorina Tessmann
Layout/technische Umsetzung: krauß-verlagsservice, Ederheim/Hürnheim

www.cornelsen.de

1. Auflage 2021

Druck: H. Heenemann, Berlin

ISBN 978-3-589-16754-8

PEFC
PEFC/04-31-1156

PEFC zertifiziert
Dieses Produkt stammt aus nachhaltig bewirtschafteten Wäldern und kontrollierten Quellen.

www.pefc.de

CONTENT

Liebe Kolleginnen und Kollegen, liebe Leserinnen und Leser,

Lernen soll Spaß machen und ist per Definition mit Neugierde und Fragenstellen verbunden. Welches Format eignet sich da besser zur Lernlektüre als eine *Mystery Story*, eine Geschichte, die Fragen aufwirft, zum Knobeln anregt und einfach Spaß macht? Und was, wenn man dabei auch noch Grammatikphänomene erlernen, üben oder vertiefen kann?
Das vorliegende Heft greift den Trend der *Mystery Story* auf und schafft damit eine motivierende Lernumgebung für das systematische Trainieren von Textverständnis, Grammatik und kreativen Textformen. Die Geschichten bieten sich insbesondere zum Vertiefen, Üben oder Erweitern oder für Vertretungsstunden an.
Das Buch besteht aus fünf *Mystery Stories*, die jeweils durch Arbeitsblätter auf zwei Lernniveaus komplementiert werden. Alle *basic*- und *advanced*-Arbeitsblätter sind so konzipiert, dass die Besprechung beider Lernniveaus gemeinsam geschehen kann. Jedes Arbeitsblatt folgt dabei einer Dreiteilung in A CONTENT, B LANGUAGE und C BEYOND. Einige bieten auch den fakultativen Teil D ADDITIONAL CREATIVES an. In Teil A soll sichergestellt werden, dass die Lernenden die Handlung der Geschichte verstanden haben. Der Teil B ist das Herzstück des Übungsbuchs und nimmt jeweils einen grammatikalischen Schwerpunkt in den Fokus. Teil C hat die Funktion eines kreativen Schreibpools, in dem die *Mystery Stories* sprachlich und inhaltlich umgewälzt und erweitert werden. Der folgenden Übersicht können Sie die thematischen und grammatikalischen Schwerpunkte der einzelnen *Mystery Stories* entnehmen:

	Titel	**Inhaltssynopse**	**Grammatikalischer Schwerpunkt**	**Kreativer Schreibpool**
1	*Igor the Brave*	Roberts Hund Igor soll den Tisch mit dem Hamburger und Geld bewachen; doch als Robert zurückkommt, fehlt beides.	*Conditional Sentences*	Perspektivwechsel, dialogisches Schreiben, Gedicht verfassen
2	*One Ordinary Afternoon**	Danny ist ein mutiger Dachshund und nach einem Meteoriteneinschlag der einzige, der die seltsamen Gäste verstehen kann.	*Past Perfect* (Unterschied zwischen *Simple* und *Progressive Aspect* wird nicht thematisiert)	Weiterführen der Geschichte, dialogisches Schreiben, zeichnerische Verarbeitung
3	*SuperChamp**	Das teuerste und beste Pferd im Stall ist verschwunden und eine Lösegeldforderung wird gefunden. Ein Fall für Detective Debs.	*Passive*	Zeitungsinterview, Brief

4	*Too Good to be True*	Boppy ist ein alter Hase im Geschäft, als Privatdetektiv macht ihm so schnell niemand etwas vor – auch kein Fernsehstar.	*Countable and Uncountable Nouns* (der Schwerpunkt liegt hier weniger auf Grammatik, dafür mehr auf Leseverstehen und literarischer Anschlussverarbeitung)	Tagebucheintrag, Perspektivwechsel
5	*The Great Pizza Robberies**	Jeden Donnerstag wird William, der beste Angestellte bei *Joe's Pizza King*, überfallen. Was hat es damit auf sich?	*Reported Speech*	Zeitungsartikel, Zeugenaussage

Grundlegende Planungsüberlegungen zu den Übungen basierten auf neigungs- und leistungsdifferenzierten Herangehensweisen. Die mit * gekennzeichneten *Mystery Stories* eignen sich auch zur Einführung des grammatikalischen Schwerpunkts. Einige *Mystery Stories* bieten sich auch besonders gut für eine diskursive Anschlussverarbeitung an. So wird beispielsweise die Frage nach der Rechtmäßigkeit der Diebstähle in *The Great Pizza Robberies* sicherlich zu einer kontroversen Debatte führen.

Folgende Aspekte/Eigenschaften werden berücksichtigt:

1) progressiver Aufbau,
2) spielerisches und entdeckendes Lernen mit hoher Motivation durch Geschichten mit Lebensweltbezug,
3) authentische Geschichten aus muttersprachlicher Hand,
4) smarte Besprechungsmöglichkeiten beider Lernlevel, sodass Sie unaufgeregt differenzieren können,

Herzlichen Dank an das Team der Pfälzischen Landesbibliothek in Speyer, das uns mit Rat und Tat zur Seite stand – war es bei Literaturbeschaffungen oder bei der Organisation der *Jours Fixes*.

Ihnen und Ihren Schülerinnen und Schülern wünschen wir viel Spaß und Erfolg mit diesem Heft. Mögen Sie genauso viel Freude und Lernerfolge mit den *Mystery Stories* haben wie wir.

Sebastian Beckmann, Bill Lowenburg und Carina Welsch
Speyer, Stroudsburg (Pennsylvania) und Maikammer, August 2020

IGOR THE BRAVE

One afternoon, Robert is very hungry and takes a walk to the sandwich shop. He takes along his pet Great Dane, Igor the Brave. Igor is usually well-behaved, which is a good thing, because Igor weighs 90 kg and Robert only weighs 50. At the sandwich shop, there is a "No Dogs" sign in the window. Igor must wait outside by the sidewalk tables.

"Stay here," Robert tells Igor. "Guard the table."

"Woof," Igor replies in his deep voice. Translation: "Okay, I got this."

Robert goes inside the shop and orders a hamburger from Suzy. Robert thinks Suzy is cute. In fact, Robert has a crush on Suzy, but he is too shy to tell her. Additionally, Suzy is taller than Robert, which does not work in his favor. He pays for his hamburger with a twenty-dollar bill and leaves a five dollar tip in the jar. He thinks, "If I leave a good tip, maybe Suzy will think I'm a big spender."

Returning to the table, Robert places his hamburger on top of the bills he received in change.

"I'm going back to get my drink," he tells Igor. "Guard my sandwich and the money."

"Ok, I got this," Igor replies. "I mean, 'woof'."

Robert goes back inside and wants to flirt with Suzy, but he's too shy. "If only I were six inches taller," he thinks. Robert pretends to carefully study the soft drink cooler for a long time before making his choice. All of a sudden, he hears Igor barking loudly outside. Running out to the sidewalk, Robert sees that both his hamburger and his money have disappeared.

Robert looks at Igor.

"I'm disappointed in you. I thought you said you would guard the table!"

"Woof," Igor replies, sheepishly.

"Is that all you can say?" Robert demands.

"Woof."

"Some guard dog you are," Robert cries, "I'm going back inside. If they have a security camera, maybe we will be able to identify the thief."

Robert asks Suzy whether the shop has a security camera.

"Yes, we do," Suzy tells him and they watch the playback of the last ten minutes. On the computer screen, we see Igor gobbling[1] up both the hamburger AND the money.

"Some guard dog," Robert says. "I thought he was barking at the thief. I wonder what he was really barking at?"

On the screen we see a lady walking her pet Chihuahua down the sidewalk past Igor and the tables.

"Now I get it," Robert says.

"That's Mrs. Trinkenschuh," Suzy says. "And her dog, Zsa-Zsa. They come in the shop often."

"Well, thanks," Robert tells Suzy. "I guess I need to order another hamburger."

"Don't worry," Suzy replies. "It's on the house."

---

1 (to) gobble: (to) eat very quickly

Robert returns to the table outside to wait for his hamburger. He is embarrassed. Mrs. Trinkenschuh and Zsa-Zsa approach, returning from their walk. Zsa-Zsa, by the way, weighs 2 kg. As Zsa-Zsa approaches, Igor the Brave lies down on the sidewalk and covers his eyes with his paws.

"How cute!" says Mrs. Trinkenschuh, passing by. "What's your dog's name?"

"He used to be Igor the Brave," Robert replies, "but I'm changing it to Igor the Shy."

Robert goes back to the sandwich counter to pick up his second hamburger.

"You look discouraged," Suzie tells him. "What's the matter?"

"Two things," Robert replies. "The first is, Igor is undependable. The second, I can't tell you."

"That's not fair," says Suzie. "You can't just tell half the story."

"If I tell you, you'll think I'm a fool," Robert says.

"No, I'll think you're a fool if you don't!"

"In that case," Robert says, "I might as well tell you. I was going to ask you to go to the movies."

"Well … why didn't you?" Suzie replies.

"I'm not sure," Robert lies. "But if I had asked, would you have said yes?"

"Sure, why not? But only if you actually ask."

"Ok, will you go to the movies with me?"

"Yes, on one condition," Suzie says. "Igor stays home."

ACTIVITIES – BASIC LEVEL

A CONTENT

A.1 Something is wrong here!

Correct the following sentences. *Korrigiere die folgenden Sätze.*

1. At the end of the story, Robert refers to his dog as Igor the Strong.

____

2. Igor is a small and tiny pet.

____

3. Dogs are not allowed at the sandwich shop.

____

4. Suzy does not want to go out with Robert.

____

5. Zsa-Zsa is Mr. Trinkenschuh's dog.

____

A.2 Igor the Brave, Robert the Shy – or the other way around?

The story is called Igor the Brave and we learn that Robert is shy. In the end, it is the other way around. Explain why.

Die Geschichte heißt Igor the Brave und wir erfahren in der Geschichte, dass Robert schüchtern ist. Am Ende ist es genau andersherum. Erkläre, wieso das der Fall ist.

____

____

____

____

____

____

Sebastian Beckmann, Bill Lowenburg, Carina Welsch · Englisch-Krimi 7/8 | 978-3-589-16754-8 | Illustration Lupe: shutterstock/Sonya illustration; Hintergrund: shutterstock/Tobias Steinert

B LANGUAGE

B.1 It's a match!

Match the type of conditional, the example sentence, and the meaning for each of them.

Verbinde die Elemente in der Tabelle.

Type 1	If Robert had asked Suzy, she would have gone out with him.	unwahrscheinlich (Gegenwart oder Zukunft)
Type 2	If Robert asks Suzy, she will go out with him.	unmöglich, nicht mehr erfüllbar (Vergangenheit)
Type 3	If Robert asked Suzy, she would go out with him.	real, möglich, erfüllbar (Gegenwart oder Zukunft)

B.2 The three ifs …

a) For each of the sentences, choose the correct verb and underline it.

Unterstreiche in jedem der folgenden Sätze die richtige Verbform.

1. If Robert was six inches taller, ***he would not be/he will not be*** so shy.
2. If we are hungry, ***we will eat/we would eat*** a sandwich, too.
3. If Robert ***hadn't taken/didn't take*** so long with the drinks, he wouldn't have had problems with his sandwich.

b) Fill in the missing verb in the correct form (Type 1–3).

Schreibe die fehlenden Verben in der richtigen Form in die Lücken.

4. If you tell Igor to watch the table, he ______________________ (to do) it even on bad days.
5. If Robert had asked Suzy earlier, she ______________________ (to say) yes.
6. If Zsa-Zsa ______________________ (to be/not) so cute, Igor wouldn't cover his face with his paws.

Now you: Have fun finishing the following sentences ☺.

If I had a dog/cat, his/her name ______________________ (to be) ______________________.

If I were Robert, I ______________________ (to watch) with Suzy.

Sebastian Beckmann, Bill Lowenburg, Carina Welsch · Englisch-Krimi 7/8 | 978-3-589-16754-8 | Illustration Lupe: shutterstock/Sonya illustration; Hintergrund: shutterstock/Tobias Steinert

B.3 What if?

The story could have taken a different direction at several points. Have a look at the sentences from the story and complete them. Use the third conditional.

An mehreren Stellen könnte die Geschichte auch andere Wendungen nehmen. Schau dir die Sätze unten an und vervollständige sie mit dem third conditional.

a. In fact, Robert has a crush on Suzy, but he is too shy to tell her.

If Robert ________________ (to be/not) too shy, he ________________ (to tell) Suzy that he has a crush on her.

b. "I'm going to get my drink," he tells Igor. "Guard my sandwich and the money."

If Robert ________________ (to go) to get his drink, Igor ________________ (to have to/not) guard the sandwich and the money.

c. Robert pretends to carefully study the soft drink cooler for a long time before making his choice. All of a sudden, he hears Igor barking loudly outside.

If Robert ________________ (to take/not) such a long time to choose his drink, the sandwich and money ________________ (to be/still) there.

d. "I'm disappointed in you. I thought you said you would guard the table."

If Igor ________________ (to guard) the table, Robert ________________ (to be/not) disappointed.

e. Robert asks Suzy whether the shop has a security camera.

If the shop ________________ (to have/not) a security camera, they ________________ (to find out/not) about Mrs. Trinkenschuh and Zsa-Zsa.

Sebastian Beckmann, Bill Lowenburg, Carina Welsch • Englisch-Krimi 7/8 | 978-3-589-16754-8 | Illustration Lupe: shutterstock/Sonya illustration; Hintergrund: shutterstock/Tobias Steinert

C BEYOND – Choose one!

C.1 Igor's point of view

Write at least four sentences from Igor's point of view. Include at least two different types of conditionals. You can use the following sentence starters.

Versetze dich in Igors Position. Schreibe mindestens vier Sätze aus seiner Sicht und verwende mindestens zwei verschiedene conditional-Formen. Du kannst die unten stehenden Satzanfänge benutzen.

Today was a very exciting / interesting / great / sad day because ...
I really like small dogs / Zsa-Zsa / Robert because ...
If Robert / Zsa-Zsa / I ... / If I were Robert / Zsa-Zsa / ..., I...

___

___

___

___

___

___

___

C.2 Robert, Suzy, and their first date

One week after the incident, Robert and Suzy go out on a date. What could they say and talk about? Write a short dialogue (at least six sentences). For ideas, you can use the words from the box.

Eine Woche nach den Ereignissen treffen sich Robert und Suzy zu einem Date. Schreibe einen Dialog zwischen den beiden. Was könnten sie sagen, worüber könnten sie sprechen? Die Wörter in der Box können dir helfen.

pleasure • (to) take a seat • (to) remember the incident • fate [= Schicksal] • (to) make plans • (to) become friends • (to) get together

Start like this: Robert: Hello, Suzy! Great to see you again!
Suzy: Hello! You too! What an *interesting* day that was last week ...

Sebastian Beckmann, Bill Lowenburg, Carina Welsch · Englisch-Krimi 7/8 | 978-3-589-16754-8 | Illustration Lupe: shutterstock/Sonya illustration; Hintergrund: shutterstock/Tobias Steinert

ACTIVITIES – ADVANCED LEVEL

A CONTENT

A.1 Something is wrong here.

Correct the following sentences. *Korrigiere die folgenden Sätze.*

1. At the end of the story, Robert refers to his dog as Igor the Strong.

2. Igor is a small and tiny pet.

3. Dogs are not allowed at the sandwich shop.

4. Suzy does not want to go out with Robert.

5. Zsa-Zsa is Mr. Trinkenschuh's dog.

A.2 Igor the Brave, Robert the Shy – or the other way around?

The story is called Igor the Brave and we learn that Robert is shy. In the end, it is the other way around. Explain why. *Die Geschichte heißt Igor the Brave und wir erfahren in der Geschichte, dass Robert schüchtern ist. Am Ende ist es genau andersherum. Erkläre, wieso das der Fall ist.*

____

____

B LANGUAGE

B.1 It's a match!

Match the sentence parts. *Verbinde die Elemente in der Tabelle.*

Type 1	If Robert had asked Suzy,	she will go out with him.	The situation is unlikely or impossible (present or future).
Type 2	If Robert asks Suzy,	she would have gone out with him.	The situation is impossible (past).
Type 3	If Robert asked Suzy,	she would go out with him.	The situation is possible (present or future).

Sebastian Beckmann, Bill Lowenburg, Carina Welsch • Englisch-Krimi 7/8 | 978-3-589-16754-8 | Illustration Lupe: shutterstock/Sonya illustration; Hintergrund: shutterstock/Tobias Steinert

B.2 The three ifs …

a) For each of the sentences, fill in the missing verb in the correct form.
Schreibe die fehlenden Verben in der richtigen Form in die Lücken.

1. If Robert was six inches taller, he ______________ (to be) so shy.
2. If we are hungry, we ______________ (to eat) a sandwich, too.
3. If Robert ______________ (to take) so long with the drinks, he wouldn't have had problems with his sandwich.

b) Choose one of the verbs in the box to complete the sentences with the correct form (Type 1–3). *Wähle für jeden Satz das passende Verb aus der Box und fülle die Lücken mit der richtigen Form des jeweiligen Verbs.*

to be • to do • to say

4. If you tell Igor to watch the table, he ______________ (to do) it even on bad days.
5. If Robert had asked Suzy earlier, she ______________ (to say) yes.
6. If Zsa-Zsa ______________ (to be) so cute, Igor wouldn't cover his face with his paws.

Now you: Finish the following sentences. Use the correct verb forms.

If I had a dog/cat, his/her came would be ______________.

If I were Robert, I would watch ______________ with Suzy.

B.3 What if?

The story could have gone a different direction at several points. Have a look at the sentences from the story and complete them. Use the third conditional.
An mehreren Stellen könnte die Geschichte auch andere Wendungen nehmen. Schau dir die Sätze unten an und vervollständige sie mit dem third conditional.

a. In fact, Robert has a crush on Suzy, but he is too shy to tell her.

If Robert ______________ (to be/not) too shy, he ______________ (to tell) Suzy that he has a crush on her.

Sebastian Beckmann, Bill Lowenburg, Carina Welsch · Englisch-Krimi 7/8 | 978-3-589-16754-8 | Illustration Lupe: shutterstock/Sonya illustration; Hintergrund: shutterstock/Tobias Steinert

b. "I'm going to get my drink", he tells Igor. "Guard my sandwich and the money."

If Robert ______________ (to go) to get his drink, Igor ______________ (to have to/not) guard the sandwich and the money.

c. Robert pretends to carefully study the soft drink cooler for a long time before making his choice. All of a sudden, he hears Igor barking loudly outside.

If Robert ______________ (to take/not) such a long time to choose his drink, ______________

____

______________ (to be) ______________

____

d. "I'm disappointed in you. I thought you said you would guard the table."

If Igor ______________ (to guard) the table,

Robert ______________________________

____

____

e. Robert asks Suzy whether the shop has a security camera. "Yes, we do."

If the shop ______________ (to have/not) a security camera, they ______________

____

____

C BEYOND – Choose one!

C.1 Igor's point of view

Write at least four sentences from Igor's point of view. Include at least two different types of conditionals.

Versetze dich in Igors Position. Schreibe mindestens vier Sätze aus seiner Sicht und verwende mindestens zwei verschiedene conditionals.

C.2 Robert, Suzy, and their first date

One week after the incident, Robert and Suzy go out on a date. What could they say and talk about? Write a short dialogue (at least six sentences). You can use the words from the box for ideas.

Eine Woche nach den Ereignissen treffen sich Robert und Suzy zu einem Date. Schreibe einen Dialog zwischen den beiden. Was könnten sie sagen, worüber könnten sie sprechen? Die Wörter in der Box können dir helfen.

pleasure • (to) take a seat • (to) remember the incident • fate [= Schicksal] • (to) make plans • (to) become friends • (to) get together

Sebastian Beckmann, Bill Lowenburg, Carina Welsch · Englisch-Krimi 7/8 | 978-3-589-16754-8 | Illustration Lupe: shutterstock/Sonya illustration; Hintergrund: shutterstock/Tobias Steinert

ONE ORDINARY[1] AFTERNOON AT OSCAR'S HOUSE

I had known Danny for a long time when a meteorite crash made me get to know him better. There was a huge boom as the hot rock from space blasted[1] through the roof, the floor upstairs and the floor of the living room next to me. I could hear it bouncing[2] around in the basement as it destroyed my collection of antiques[3] and shattered every bottle of the home-made elderberry[4] wine I had wanted to give to my best friends.

Danny, my fearless Dachshund, ran downstairs to investigate. Danny is not afraid of anything. He tasted the elderberry wine on the basement floor and decided that he liked it. After I had gathered enough courage to go down to the basement, Danny was already a little tipsy[5].

The meteorite looked like a fist-sized piece of stone. It had traveled billions of miles across the galaxy, only to come to rest in my basement. There it sat, in a puddle of elderberry wine, creating a cloud of steam. The steam actually smelled pretty good. I had planned to go out on a date that evening, but now it appeared the date was out of the question.

"What should I do now?" I blurted[6] out.

"You might want to call the Fire Department," Danny replied. "That thing is hot." Danny usually didn't talk much, except when he had something important to say.

"Good idea," I said, adding, "Go easy on that wine."

The meteorite sat in the puddle, glowing. It also made a strange noise. The noise sounded like a type of music, but not any music I had ever heard.

"How can a meteorite make music?" I asked Danny.

"I don't know," he replied, "but it's got a good beat and you can dance to it." He demonstrated a few very cool moves.

The meteorite continued to glow. It was easy to see why: It had passed through Earth's atmosphere at 160,000 miles per hour. Luckily, the elderberry wine had cooled it off, but only slightly.

Suddenly, I heard sirens and the house was surrounded by fire trucks. Firemen barged[7] in the front door and ran down into the basement. I hurried outside to talk to the Fire Chief. He told me the neighbors had seen steam rising through the new hole in my roof and had called the fire department.

Just then, a television crew arrived. Several cameramen and a young woman reporter rushed out of their van.

---

1 (to) blast: The meteorite exploded and created a hole.
2 (to) bounce: A ball bounces around if you throw it on the ground.
3 antiques (n): old objects
4 elderberry (n): *Holunder*
5 tipsy (a): a little drunk
6 (to) blurt: (to) say very suddenly, without thinking
7 (to) barge: They entered the house fast.

"What happened?" the reporter asked.

"Ask him," the Fire Chief said, pointing to me.

"Well?" the reporter asked, "What happened? Tell our viewers!"

"I had just lay down for a nap and then, Ka-BOOM! No nap! Who called you, anyway?"

"Someone named Danny," she replied. "He had a funny-sounding voice."

By this time, a crowd of neighbors had gathered around the house. Then the police arrived.

To add to the confusion, Danny ran out and began barking at everyone. The police ordered the crowd to move away and set up barriers.

"What's going on here?" the police officer demanded. Her name tag said Sergeant Schmidt. She appeared to be in a bad mood.

"Meteorite in the basement," the Fire Chief calmly explained, as if it were an everyday event.

"Are you crazy?" yelled Sergeant Schmidt.

"See for yourself," replied the Fire Chief.

"Come on, I'll show you," I said, starting toward the house.

"You can't go back in there!" Sergeant Schmidt yelled, louder than before.

"But I have a date tonight." I pleaded. "I have to get ready."

"Are you crazy?" she said. It appeared to be her favorite question.

Just then, one of the firefighters stuck his head out of the doorway.

"Hey, Chief, come right away! You have to see this!"

We all ran into the house. There, down in the basement, we encountered a strange sight on the floor.

The firemen had just finished hosing down the meteorite and it was finally cool. Water was everywhere.

A small door opened on the side of the meteorite. Out popped two tiny alien astronauts wearing space suits. They were about one inch[8] tall. They walked around, waving their arms excitedly, speaking a strange language we humans could not understand.

"They are apologizing," Danny explained. Apparently, he had no trouble understanding. Everyone else was in such a state of shock that they did not appear surprised by a talking dog.

"They said they had been on their way to Jupiter," Danny continued, "and took a wrong turn at Mars. Then they ran out of fuel and crash landed here on Earth."

"Is there anything we can do to help them?" I asked.

Danny barked at the little spacemen and they said something back to him.

"They say they are able to extract hydrogen from the water provided by the nice firemen. In a few minutes they will be ready to continue their journey."

"They cannot leave!" shouted Sergeant Schmidt. "We must notify the government! This could be an invasion!"

Danny barked a message at the little men and the two tiny astronauts began to laugh. They laughed so hard they were rolling on the floor. One of them stood up and said something to Danny.

"What did he say?" demanded Sergeant Schmidt.

Danny replied: "He said: are you crazy? We would never invade Earth! We love all the other species on this planet, but you humans are too primitive! Too difficult! We just want to get out of here! We're already late!"

8 One inch = 2.54 centimeters

Sebastian Beckmann, Bill Lowenburg, Carina Welsch · Englisch-Krimi 7/8 | 978-3-589-16754-8 | Illustration Lupe: shutterstock/Sonya illustration; Hintergrund: shutterstock/Tobias Steinert

"Late for what?" I asked.

"For the video game tournament on Jupiter," Danny explained. "That had been their destination."

Sergeant Schmidt pulled out her mobile phone and began to punch in a number. The tiny alien astronaut pointed a tiny ray gun at her and a flash of light froze her in place.

"Don't worry," Danny assured everyone. "It's only temporary."

"What about all this damage to my house?" I said to Danny. "Ask him about that."

The dachshund and the mini-astronauts conferred.[9]

"They will fix everything with their proton beam[10]," Danny replied. "He guarantees, all will be restored to the way it had been."

"What about the TV crew and the neighbors?" I asked.

"No problem," Danny said. "Everyone's memory will be erased."

The spaceman zapped[11] Sergeant Schmidt and the firemen with his ray gun. They all turned to leave the basement.

"Have a nice day," Sergeant Schmidt said, as if in a dream. "I'm going for coffee."

Outside, the neighbors and TV crew had gone away. The police and fire crew got into their vehicles and drove off.

Danny and I watched the little rock-shaped spacecraft float through the hole in the roof. The hole sealed[12] itself up and it looked like nothing had ever happened. We watched the tiny ship rise into the sky until it disappeared.

"Will they erase our memory, too?" I asked Danny.

"I don't think so," he said.

"Why not?" I wondered.

Danny looked up at me.

"Are you crazy? Who would ever believe us?"

9 (to) confer: (to) talk to each other
10 proton beam (n): *Protonenstrahl*
11 (to) zap: (to) hit/(to) shoot
12 (to) seal: (to) close

ONE ORDINARY AFTERNOON – BASIC LEVEL

A LANGUAGE

A.1 Do aliens really exist?

a) True or false?
Correct the false statements.
Richtig oder falsch? Korrigiere die falschen Aussagen.

	Statement	True	False
1	Danny can talk to humans.		
2	Danny can talk to the strange astronauts.		
3	The Fire Chief talks to the aliens.		
4	Sergeant Schmidt has a ray gun.		
5	Danny is a cat.		
6	There is a television crew at the scene.		

Now you: come up with at least four true or false questions for your partner and swap your questions with him/her. Correct the false statements.
Jetzt bist du dran: Schreibe selbst mindestens vier Aussagen für deinen Partner/deine Partnerin auf. Tauscht dann eure Fragen und verbessert die falschen Aussagen.

b) What's going on at Oscar's house?
Write the answer for each of the following questions on the lines below.
Schreibe die Antworten für die folgenden Fragen auf die Linie.

1. For how long had Oscar known Danny?

____

2. What are the details on the object that crashed into the house?

____

3. Who is Danny and what is his special ability?

____

4. Why could the visitors not leave the place?

____

 | Sebastian Beckmann, Bill Lowenburg, Carina Welsch · Englisch-Krimi 7/8 | 978-3-589-16754-8 |
Illustration: o. r.: Dorina Tessmann; Lupe: shutterstock/Sonya illustration; Hintergrund: shutterstock/Tobias Steinert

A.2 Not so ordinary after all...

What makes this afternoon not as ordinary as the title of the story might suggest?
Explain in less than four sentences.

Dieser Nachmittag ist nicht so normal, wie der Titel der Geschichte suggeriert.
Erkläre in weniger als vier Sätzen, warum das der Fall ist.

____

____

____

____

B LANGUAGE

B.1 One ordinary past sentence

a) Match the sentence parts.

Verbinde die Satzhälften.

1. The meteorite destroyed the wine	a. that the neighbors had seen smoke.
2. After I had gathered enough courage	b. I had been saving for special occasions.
3. I had planned to go on a date	c. but nothing I had ever heard before.
4. The noise sounded like music	d. I went downstairs to find Danny tipsy.
5. The Fire Chief told me	e. but this appeared to be out of the question.

b) Write sentences!

For each Simple Past sentence below, complete the second sentence in the Past Perfect. Then, underline the different parts: the part with the action that happens first with a blue pencil, the action that happens afterwards with a red pencil.

Ergänze in den folgenden Sätzen das Past Perfect. Entscheide, welcher Teil zuerst und welcher danach passiert ist. Unterstreiche dann den Teil, der zuerst passiert ist, mit einem blauen Stift und den Teil mit dem, was danach passiert ist, mit einem roten Stift.

The people came to see what happened. A meteorite ____________________ (to crash) into the house. The firemen came because a neighbor ____________________ (to call) them. The astronauts explained they would repair Oscar's house.

He ____________________ (to ask) them about the damage.

Sebastian Beckmann, Bill Lowenburg, Carina Welsch · Englisch-Krimi 7/8 | 978-3-589-16754-8 | Illustration Lupe: shutterstock/Sonya illustration; Hintergrund: shutterstock/Tobias Steinert

B.2 Oscar had Danny for a long time

Complete the sentences below with the correct form of the verbs.

Vervollständige die Sätze mit den korrekten Verbformen.

He ___had___ (to have) a lot of elderberry wine.

He ___had wanted___ (to want) to give the wine to his best friends.

The meteorite ______________ (to come) to rest in the basement.

It ______________ (to travel) billions of miles.

There ______________ (to be) a lot of people outside the house.

They ______________ (to come) to the house to find out more about the crash.

The video game tournament ______________ (to take place) on Jupiter.

Registration ______________ (to end) three weeks before.

You could not see the hole anymore. It ______________ (to seal) itself.

C BEYOND – CHOOSE ONE!

C.1 They continue their journey.

Imagine you know how the story continues. Where do the alien astronauts fly next and who do they meet? Write a minimum of 8–10 sentences and use at least 3 past perfect (with simple past) constructions. *Stell Dir vor, wir können herausfinden, wie die Geschichte weitergeht. Wohin fliegen die Alien-Astronauten als nächstes und wen treffen sie? Schreibe mindestens 8–10 Sätze und verwende dabei mindestens 3 Past Perfect mit Simple Past-Sätzen.*

Start like this: After they had left with their meteorite, …

____

____

____

____

____

____

____

____

Sebastian Beckmann, Bill Lowenburg, Carina Welsch · Englisch-Krimi 7/8 | 978-3-589-16754-8 | Illustration Lupe: shutterstock/Sonya illustration; Hintergrund: shutterstock/Tobias Steinert

C.2 Give them words.

Come up with a dialogue between the two aliens. What do they think about their quick stop on Earth? The words in the box can help you.

Denk dir einen Dialog zwischen den beiden Außerirdischen aus. Was denken sie über ihren kurzen Halt auf der Erde? Die Wörter in der Box helfen dir, falls du Ideen brauchst.

funny • strange • talking animals • houses • wine

Sebastian Beckmann, Bill Lowenburg, Carina Welsch · Englisch-Krimi 7/8 | 978-3-589-16754-8 | Illustration Lupe: shutterstock/Sonya illustration; Hintergrund: shutterstock/Tobias Steinert

ONE ORDINARY AFTERNOON – ADVANCED LEVEL

A LANGUAGE

A.1 Do aliens really exist?

a) True or false?
Correct the false statements.
Richtig oder falsch? Korrigiere die falschen Aussagen.

	Statement	True	False
1	Danny can talk to humans.		
2	Danny can talk to the strange astronauts.		
3	The Fire Chief talks to the aliens.		
4	Sergeant Schmidt has a ray gun.		
5	Danny is a cat.		
6	There is a television crew at the scene.		

Now you: come up with at least four true or false questions for your partner and swap your questions with him/her. Correct the false statements.
Jetzt bist du dran: Schreibe selbst mindestens vier Aussagen für deinen Partner/deine Partnerin auf. Tauscht sie dann aus und verbessert die falschen Aussagen.

b) What's going on at Oscar's house?
Write the answer for each of the following questions on the lines below.
Schreibe die Antworten für die folgenden Fragen auf die Linie.

1. For how long had Oscar known Danny?

____

2. What are the details on the object that crashed into the house?

____

3. Who is Danny and what is his special ability?

____

4. Why could the visitors not leave the place?

____

Für inhaltliche Veränderungen durch Dritte übernimmt der Verlag keine Verantwortung. | Sebastian Beckmann, Bill Lowenburg, Carina Welsch · Englisch-Krimi 7/8 | 978-3-589-16754-8 |
Illustration: o. r.: Dorina Tessmann; Lupe: shutterstock/Sonya illustration; Hintergrund: shutterstock/Tobias Steinert

A.2 Not so ordinary after all...

What makes this afternoon not as ordinary as the title of the story might suggest? Explain in less than four sentences.

Dieser Nachmittag ist nicht so normal wie der Titel der Geschichte suggeriert. Erkläre in weniger als vier Sätzen, warum das der Fall ist.

____

____

____

____

B LANGUAGE

B.1 One ordinary past sentence.

a) Match the sentence parts.

Verbinde die Satzhälften.

1. The meteorite destroyed the wine	a. that the neighbors had seen smoke.
2. After I had gathered enough courage	b. I had been saving for special occasions.
3. I had planned to go on a date	c. but nothing I had ever heard before.
4. The noise sounded like music	d. I went downstairs to find Danny tipsy.
5. The Fire Chief told me	e. but this appeared to be out of the question.

b) Write sentences.

For each Simple Past sentence below, complete the second sentence in the Past Perfect. Then, underline the different parts: the part with the action that happens first with a blue pencil, the action that happens afterwards with a red pencil.

Schau dir die folgenden Sätze an und entscheide, welcher Teil zuerst, welcher danach passiert ist. Schreibe nun je einen vollständigen Satz im simple past und past perfect. Unterstreiche dann den Teil, der zuerst passiert ist, mit einem blauen Stift und den Teil mit dem, was danach passiert ist, mit einem roten Stift.

The people came to see what happened. A meteorite ________________ (to crash) into the house. The firemen came because a neighbor ________________. (to call/them) The astronauts explained they would repair Oscar's house. ________________ ________________________. (to ask/he/about the damage)

Sebastian Beckmann, Bill Lowenburg, Carina Welsch · Englisch-Krimi 7/8 | 978-3-589-16754-8 | Illustration Lupe: shutterstock/Sonya illustration; Hintergrund: shutterstock/Tobias Steinert

B.2 Oscar had known Danny for a long time.

Complete the sentences below with the correct form of the verbs in the box.

Vervollständige die Sätze mit den korrekten Verbformen aus der Box.

to travel • to seal • to play • to come • to be • to end • to come • to come • to sing • to take place

He ___had___ a lot of elderberry wine. ([to] have)

He ___had wanted___ to give the wine to his best friends. ([to] want)

The meteorite ______________ to rest in the basement.

It ______________ billions of miles.

There ______________ a lot of people outside the house.

They ______________ to the house to find out more about the crash.

The video game tournament ______________ on Jupiter.

Registration ______________ three weeks before.

You could not see the hole anymore. It ______________ itself.

C BEYOND – CHOOSE ONE!

C.1 They continue their journey.

Imagine you know how the story continues. Where do the alien astronauts fly next and who do they meet? Write a minimum of 8–10 sentences and use at least 3 past perfect (with simple past) constructions.

Stell Dir vor, wir können herausfinden, wie die Geschichte weitergeht. Wohin fliegen die Alien-Astronauten als nächstes und wen treffen sie? Schreibe mindestens 8–10 Sätze und verwende dabei mindestens 3 Past Perfect mit Simple Past-Sätzen.

Start like this: After they had left with their meteorite, …

____

____

____

____

Sebastian Beckmann, Bill Lowenburg, Carina Welsch · Englisch-Krimi 7/8 | 978-3-589-16754-8 | Illustration Lupe: shutterstock/Sonya illustration; Hintergrund: shutterstock/Tobias Steinert

C.2 Give them words.

Come up with a dialogue between the two aliens. What do they think about their quick stop on Earth? The words in the box can help you.

Denk dir einen Dialog zwischen den beiden Außerirdischen aus. Was denken sie über ihren kurzen Halt auf der Erde? Die Wörter in der Box helfen dir, falls du Ideen brauchst.

funny • strange • talking animals • houses • wine

Sebastian Beckmann, Bill Lowenburg, Carina Welsch • Englisch-Krimi 7/8 | 978-3-589-16754-8 | Illustration Lupe: shutterstock/Sonya illustration; Hintergrund: shutterstock/Tobias Steinert

SUPERCHAMP, WHERE ARE YOU?

Impossible. How could the world's most famous racehorse go missing? That is what everyone was asking the day after SuperChamp disappeared. How could a thief ever hide a beautiful bay horse, a horse whose picture had been shown in every newspaper over the past year? Within days, SuperChamp would be recognized. However, by then it might be too late and the horse might have been hurt – or worse.

It happened like this. Following his morning training session, SuperChamp was put out to graze with the other horses. Their pasture stretched for many acres over the countryside and sometimes the horses roamed[1] far out of sight from their luxurious paddock. In the evening when the horses returned to the paddock, SuperChamp was not among them. Mr. Irving, who owned SuperChamp, knew who to call.

Detective Deborah Debs and her 3D Detective Agency were called by Mr. Irving. It turned out that this was a perfect case for Debs. Despite her unusual background as a hairdresser and beauty stylist, in recent years Debs had become famous by solving case after case that had confused the police, as well as Scotland Yard and Interpol. When time allowed, her beauty shop was still opened on weekends, mainly because she enjoyed gossiping with her friends.

Detective Debs also had the advantage of being very short, standing just under five feet in height and weighing 99 pounds. Along with her small stature, she appeared disorganized and scatterbrained[2]. This, of course, was not true in reality and it was very effective. She was not taken seriously by many people. They assumed she was not paying attention or even forgot she was present, and sometimes revealed information they later wished they hadn't.

Now in spite of her appearance, Detective Debs was a dangerous enemy for criminals. Not only was she a black belt in Ju-Jitsu, she was the reigning UK Pistol Champion for each of the past ten years. Her IQ was 138. She read a dozen books a month and slept only four hours per night. She was not an individual to be messed with.

Arriving at the Irving Estate late in the afternoon, Detective Debs was shown to the paddock by a very pretty young woman with an accent. Debs appeared quite out of place in her raincoat, high-top sneakers, and rather ridiculous hat. She carried a large handbag.

1 (to) roam: (to) walk around
2 scatterbrained (a): *schusselig*

"Have you received a ransom[3] note," she asked Mr. Irving. He looked exhausted.

"Nothing," he replied, his hands shaking slightly.

Detective Debs was introduced to Billy Barnes, the head trainer, by Mr. Irving. Barnes was an older man, very tall, who appeared to be in outstanding physical condition. Pacing angrily back and forth, Barnes looked to be in a rage.

"Wait till I get my hands on those thieves," Barnes snarled. "They'll regret the day they were born."

"Now Barnes," Mr. Irving said, "Try calming yourself. Detective Debs here would like to ask you a few questions."

"I've already talked to the police!" Barnes shouted. Looking down at Detective Debs, Barnes let out a rude laugh. "Why you're the size of a jockey! And you call yourself a detective?"

"Actually," replied Debs," Mr. Irving is the one calling me a detective. My name is Deborah." She extended her hand to shake. Barnes tried squeezing it hard, hoping to intimidate[4] her. Debs squeezed back harder, causing Barnes to flinch in pain. Then she released her grip.

"I'd just like you to tell me what happened," said Debs.

"Very simple," said Barnes, shaking his hand behind his back. "Twenty-one horses were let out to graze this afternoon. Twenty returned. SuperChamp was gone."

"Yes, that certainly was a very simple story, Mr. Barnes. Nothing more to tell?"

"No", said Barnes. "That's about it. I apologize for being so rude. I was angry that my prize horse has been stolen. I mean *Mr. Irving's* prize horse … Sorry, Sir." Removing his cap, Barnes made a slight bow to Mr. Irving. "I didn't mean any disrespect, Sir."

"That's quite all right, Barnes," said Mr. Irving. "I know how hard you've worked with SuperChamp and all of our other winners." Turning to Detective Debs, Mr. Irving continued. "Our horses have been trained by Barnes for twenty-five years." Despite his words, Mr. Irving appeared annoyed, which Debs noted. She continued studying Barnes more closely.

"Mr. Barnes, that's quite a head of hair you've got for a man your age," Debs remarked, trying to lighten the mood.

"Just lucky, I suppose," replied Barnes, blushing.

"And not a touch of grey," Debs continued, giggling. "Why, your hair is almost the same color as the bay[5] horses!"

"Indeed, my wife says so as well," Barnes blurted out, blushing[6] more.

"Why Mr. Barnes is actually a newlywed," interjected Mr. Irving. He just married his lovely wife this past year."

"Perhaps you'd like to meet her," Barnes said, thankful to shift the attention from himself. "She was the young lady who escorted you to the paddock earlier. Let me show you the horses and then we'll go to our cottage. My wife will make some tea."

In the paddock, Detective Debs and Mr. Irving were led down the line of stalls by Barnes. Each horse had an individual stall and they were all clean and tidy.

---

3 ransom (n): *das Lösegeld*
4 (to) intimidate: *einschüchtern*
5 A bay horse is a red brown horse.
6 (to) blush: (to) turn red

Sebastian Beckmann, Bill Lowenburg, Carina Welsch · Englisch-Krimi 7/8 | 978-3-589-16754-8 | Illustration Lupe: shutterstock/Sonya illustration; Hintergrund: shutterstock/Tobias Steinert

"We pay attention to every detail," Barnes explained proudly. "For example, now in the early evening, we keep the lighting low so the horses know the day is ending and they can relax."

"Remarkable," said Debs as she looked first at one horse and then another, working her way down the paddock. "They're all so big and strong that I feel like an insect. Plus, a lot of them look alike to me. How can you tell a winner?"

"It takes experience," Barnes said, with a slight touch of anger in his voice. "Why don't we go have our tea?"

"Before we do," said Debs, "I'll need to see SuperChamp's stall."

"Why certainly," Barnes replied, leading her there. "Only there isn't much to see. It's empty." He sighed[7].

Debs pulled a tape measure, a flashlight, and magnifying glass from her handbag. She began performing a thorough[8] inspection of SuperChamp's stall. First, she measured the size of the stall and double-checked all her measurements, writing them carefully in a notebook. Next, she began collecting samples[9] from the feed tray, the straw on the floor, and the water trough[10]. Finally, she documented everything by taking a great number of photos from many different positions. It took a very long time.

Billy Barnes began being fidgeting[11] and left for the cottage, saying he would have his wife put on the tea. Mr. Irving looked really exhausted[12].

"I've got to get some dinner," Mr. Irving told Debs. "I haven't eaten all day. Stay here as long as you need to."

"I just need one more piece of evidence," Debs replied. "Stop over at Barnes' cottage after dinner."

As soon as Mr. Irving left, Detective Debs turned up the lights and had a more thorough look at the horses. The lights were turned back down and Debs proceeded to the Barnes' cottage.

One hour later, Mr. Irving entered the cottage. There were signs of a mighty struggle. Furniture was overturned and broken dishes were all over the floor. He was shocked to see Mr. and Mrs. Barnes each securely handcuffed to a heavy chair with a gag[13] stuffed in their mouth. Detective Debs was sitting by the fireplace enjoying a cup of tea.

"What on earth!" cried Mr. Irving.

"Here are the guilty people," said Debs. "Care for some tea?"

Mr. Irving struggled for words.

"But … how? Why? And where is SuperChamp?"

"I'll let Mr. Barnes explain. As for SuperChamp, he's over in the paddock, hoping to have his face washed. He's been there all along. He never left the estate."

Debs pulled the gag out of Mr. Barnes' mouth. The words poured out.

"All these years I've been training your horses and earning you millions! And you pay me almost nothing! It was time to get even, you *Cheapskate*[14]!"

Debs stuffed the gag back in Barnes' mouth.

---

7 (to) sigh: *seufzen*
8 thorough: careful
9 samples (n): hier: *die Spuren*
10 trough (n): The horses drink out of troughs.
11 (to) fidget: *herumzappeln*
12 exhausted (a): really tired
13 gag (n): *der Knebel*
14 cheapskate (n): a person who does not like to spend money

Sebastian Beckmann, Bill Lowenburg, Carina Welsch · Englisch-Krimi 7/8 | 978-3-589-16754-8 | Illustration Lupe: shutterstock/Sonya illustration; Hintergrund: shutterstock/Tobias Steinert

“As Mr. Barnes said earlier, the story was simple. He just didn’t tell us the *whole* story. In the afternoon, one of the other horses was brought to the forest on the far end of the estate. SuperChamp received a ‘makeover’ so he blended in with the rest of the herd in the low light of the paddock.”

“You mean he was there all the time?” Mr. Irving repeated, still trying to understand.

“Yes,” explained Debs. “In the very next stall to his own. His blaze had been covered up with the same hair dye[15] Mr. Barnes used to make himself appear younger for his wife.”

The gag was pulled from Mrs. Barnes’s mouth.

“Late tonight, we were going to ship SuperChamp to my father’s ranch in Argentina,” she said. “By raising many champion racehorses from his offspring, we could become rich! If Mr. Irving was not such a *Cheapskate* …”

“Well, there you have it,” said Debs, replacing the gag in Mrs. Barnes’ mouth.

“Brilliant, Debs!” said Mr. Irving. “By taking all those measurements and photos, you no doubt solved the case.”

“Not at all,” said Debs. “That was actually a trick. I needed to get you and Barnes out of there so I could begin examining the horses more closely. I knew what Barnes had done as soon as I saw his silly dyed hair earlier in the afternoon. I happen to know a thing or two about hair dye,” she said, pulling an envelope marked EVIDENCE from her bag and holding up the bottle.

15 hair dye (n): color you put in your hair

SUPERCHAMP, WHERE ARE YOU? – BASIC LEVEL

A CONTENT

A.1 Let's get it right!

Work on the following multiple-choice questions.
Be aware that more than one answer can be correct.

Beantworte die folgenden multiple choice-Fragen. Beachte, dass mehr als eine Antwort korrekt sein kann.

1. SuperChamp is …
   a) a horse   b) a race dog   c) a kangaroo rat   d) an animal   e) a hero

2. SuperChamp is owned by …
   a) Mr. Barnes   b) Detective Debs   c) Mrs. Miller   d) Mr. Irving   e) Mrs. Barnes

3. Mr. Barnes is …
   a) SuperChamp's trainer   b) a police officer   c) the kidnapper   d) Deb's friend
   e) a priest

4. Detective Debs is …
   a) a Scotland Yard Inspector   b) a police chief   c) a beauty stylist   d) private detective
   e) a very bad shooter

5. All of the following adjectives describe Debs EXCEPT:
   a) tall   b) short   c) strong   d) smart   e) not very intelligent

A.2 Who is who?

Draw a character chart of the people in the story on an extra sheet of paper and indicate their relation to one another. Add at least two facts about every character.

Zeichne eine Figurenkonstellation anhand der Geschichte. Verdeutliche auch, in welchem Verhältnis die Figuren zueinander stehen. Ergänze mindestens zwei Aspekte pro Figur.

Debs

INFO

A *character chart* helps you to get an overview of the people in a story. Write the names in boxes or circle them, then connect them with lines to show their relation/connection.

Hint: Include for example SuperChamp, Mr. Irving, …

 | Sebastian Beckmann, Bill Lowenburg, Carina Welsch · Englisch-Krimi 7/8 | 978-3-589-16754-8 |
Illustration: o. r.: Dorina Tessmann; Lupe: shutterstock/Sonya illustration; Hintergrund: shutterstock/Tobias Steinert

A.3 The missing clue...

Debs was collecting evidences to solve the case. Where had SuperChamp been and how did she find out in the end?

Debs sammelt Beweise, um den Fall zu lösen. Wo war SuperChamp und wie hat sie dies am Ende herausgefunden?

____

____

B LANGUAGE

B.1 Go and find the evidence!

a) Have a look.
Go back to the text and find the missing verbs. Fill them in.
Gehe zurück zum Text und finde die fehlenden Verben. Schreibe sie in die Lücken.

1. Detective Deborah Debs and her 3D Detective Agency ____________ ________________ by Mr. Irving (line 19).
2. "No," said Barnes. "That's about it. I apologize for being so rude. I was angry that my prize horse ____________ ____________ ____________. I mean Mr. Irving's prize horse." (lines 52–53)
3. "Yes," explained Debs. "In the very next stall to his own. His blaze ____________ ____________ ____________ up with the same hair dye Mr. Barnes used to make himself appear younger for his wife." (lines 108–109)

b) Have another look.
There are two more sentences in the passive. But this time, you have to find the gaps and the lines yourself. Find them and write them down, too.
Hier sind noch zwei weitere Sätze. Aber dieses Mal musst du die Stellen im Text selbst finden.
Schreibe die Zeilen auf, sobald du sie gefunden hast.

4. How could a thief ever hide a beautiful bay horse, a horse whose picture ____________ ____________ ____________ in every newspaper over the past year? (line ________).
5. Detective Debs ____________ ____________ to the paddock by a very young woman with an accent (line ________).

Sebastian Beckmann, Bill Lowenburg, Carina Welsch · Englisch-Krimi 7/8 | 978-3-589-16754-8 | Illustration Lupe: shutterstock/Sonya illustration; Hintergrund: shutterstock/Tobias Steinert

c) Think about it!

Have a look at the verbs from a) and b). Then fill in the different parts we need to form the passive of verbs into the boxes below.

Schau dir die Verben aus a) und b) genauer an. Schreibe dann die verschiedenen Teile, die wir für das Passiv eines Verbs brauchen, in die Kästchen.

To make a verb passive, we need:

	+	______________ (regular verbs) ______________ (irregular verbs) ▷ ______________ (expert word)

1. You often use the passive to give statistics or facts.
   2.500 cars were bought in Paris yesterday.
2. You do not use the passive to give personal or informal information.
   My brother bought a car. NOT: ~~A car was bought by my brother.~~
3. Not every sentence in the active can be put in the passive.
   Many French people live in Saarbrücken. ▷ no passive

B.2 Let's be active and passive!

a) Let's be passive!

Here are some sentences with active verbs. Rewrite them:

1. Use the passive. 2. Use the same tense as in the original.

Unten findest du einige Sätze, die aktive Formen verwenden. Schreibe diese ins Passiv um und behalte dabei die ursprüngliche Zeitform bei.

1. Mr. Irving called Detective Debs. ______________
2. Someone has stolen the prize horse. ______________
3. He introduced Debs to Billy Barnes. ______________
4. Mr. Barnes has trained the horses for 25 years. ______________

   ____
5. Extra: Within days, people would recognize SuperChamp. ______________

   ____

▷ *Tip: If you need help to get you started (with sentences 1 and 2), have a look at the sentences in B.1.*

Sebastian Beckmann, Bill Lowenburg, Carina Welsch · Englisch-Krimi 7/8 | 978-3-589-16754-8 | Illustration Lupe: shutterstock/Sonya illustration; Hintergrund: shutterstock/Tobias Steinert

b) Let's be active!

Here are some sentences with passive verbs. Rewrite them:

1. Use the active. 2. Use the same tense as in the original.

Unten findest du einige Sätze, die passive Formen verwenden.
Schreibe diese ins Aktiv um und behalte dabei die ursprüngliche Zeitform bei.

1. The gag was pulled from Mrs. Barnes' mouth by Debs.

____

____

2. Furniture was overturned in a fight by someone.

____

____

3. The lights were turned back down by Debs.

____

____

4. She was not taken seriously by many people.

____

____

5. Detective Debs was shown to the paddock by a very pretty young woman.

____

____

| Sebastian Beckmann, Bill Lowenburg, Carina Welsch · Englisch-Krimi 7/8 | 978-3-589-16754-8 |
Illustration Lupe und Detektivmütze: shutterstock/Sonya illustration; Hintergrund: shutterstock/Tobias Steinert

C BEYOND – CHOOSE ONE!

C.1 Asking Detective Debs

Imagine you are a reporter for a local newspaper. You are interviewing Detective Debs about the disappearance of SuperChamp. Write a short dialogue between the two people. You have to use at least three sentences in the passive.

Stell dir vor, du arbeitest für eine Lokalzeitung. Führe ein Interview mit Detective Debs über das Verschwinden von SuperChamp. Verwende mindestens drei Verben im Passiv.

You can start like this:

Reporter: Hello, Detective Debs. Tell us something about SuperChamp's disappearance. What happened?

Debs: Hello! SuperChamp was kidnapped, but luckily, I was able to help the owner, Mr. Irving.

Reporter: Ok let's start at the beginning… Who called you in the first place?

Debs: I …

____

____

____

____

____

____

____

____

____

____

____

____

____

____

Tip: Once you are finished, underline your passive verb forms in a color of your choice.

Tipp: Unterstreiche deine Verben im Passiv in einer Farbe deiner Wahl, sobald du fertig bist.

Sebastian Beckmann, Bill Lowenburg, Carina Welsch · Englisch-Krimi 7/8 | 978-3-589-16754-8 | Illustration Lupe: shutterstock/Sonya illustration; Hintergrund: shutterstock/Tobias Steinert

C.2 Writing a letter

After Detective Debs solves the case and Bill Barnes is taken to the police station, he writes a letter to Mr. Irving in which he explains everything he did. Imagine you are Bill and write the letter from his perspective. You have to use at least three sentences in the passive.

Nachdem Detective Debs den Fall gelöst hat und Bill Barnes zur Polizeiinspektion mitgenommen worden ist, schreibt er einen Brief an Mr. Irving, in dem er erklärt, was er getan hat und seine Gründe darlegt. Stell dir vor, du bist Bill und schreibst den Brief. Verwende mindestens drei Verben im Passiv.

Start like this: Dear Mr. Irving, …

(to) work hard • (to) train the horses • (to) earn a lot of money • (to) earn little money • bad payment • (to) be angry • (to) be treated fairly • long days, not time off • (to) appreciate someone (jemanden wertschätzen)

Tip: Once you are finished, underline your passive verb forms in a color of your choice.

Tipp: Unterstreiche deine Verben im Passiv in einer Farbe deiner Wahl, sobald du fertig bist.

Sebastian Beckmann, Bill Lowenburg, Carina Welsch · Englisch-Krimi 7/8 | 978-3-589-16754-8 | Illustration Lupe: shutterstock/Sonya illustration; Hintergrund: shutterstock/Tobias Steinert

SUPERCHAMP, WHERE ARE YOU? – ADVANCED LEVEL

A CONTENT

A.1 Let's get it right …

Work on the following multiple-choice questions.
Be aware that more than one answer can be correct.
Beantworte die folgenden multiple choice-Fragen. Beachte, dass mehr als eine Antwort korrekt sein kann.

1. SuperChamp is …
   a) a horse b) a race dog c) a kangaroo rat d) an animal e) a hero
2. SuperChamp is owned by …
   a) Mr. Barnes b) Detective Debs c) Mrs. Miller d) Mr. Irving e) Mrs. Barnes
3. Mr. Barnes is …
   a) SuperChamp's trainer b) a police officer c) the kidnapper d) Deb's friend
   e) a priest
4. Detective Debs is …
   a) a Scotland Yard Inspector b) a police chief c) a beauty stylist d) private detective
   e) a very bad shooter
5. All of the following adjectives describe Debs EXCEPT:
   a) tall b) short c) strong d) smart e) not very intelligent

A.2 Who is who?

Draw a character chart of the people in the story on an extra sheet of paper and indicate their relation to one another. Add at least two facts about every character.
Zeichne eine Figurenkonstellation anhand der Geschichte. Verdeutliche auch, wie die verschiedenen Figuren in Relation zu einander stehen. Ergänze mindestens zwei Aspekte pro Figur.

Debs

INFO

A *character chart* helps you to get an overview of the people in a story. Write the names in boxes or circle them, then connect them with lines to show their relation/connection.

A 3 The missing clue

Debs was collecting evidences to solve the case. Where had SuperChamp been and how did she find out in the end?

Debs sammelt Beweise, um den Fall zu lösen. Wo war SuperChamp und wie hat sie dies am Ende herausgefunden?

____

____

B LANGUAGE

B.1 Go and find the evidence!

a) Have a look.
Go back to the text and find the missing verbs. Fill them in.
Gehe zurück zum Text und finde die fehlenden Verben. Schreibe sie in die Lücken.

1. Detective Deborah Debs and her 3D Detective Agency ____________ ____________ by Mr. Irving (line 19).
2. "No," said Barnes. "That's about it. I apologize for being so rude. I was angry that my prize horse ____________ ____________ ____________. I mean Mr. Irving's prize horse." (lines 52–53)
3. "Yes," explained Debs. "In the very next stall to his own. His blaze ____________ ____________ ____________ up with the same hair dye Mr. Barnes used to make himself appear younger for his wife." (lines 108–109)

b) Have another look.
Now you – go back to the text and find at least one more sentence with a passive verb – or maybe you can find two? Write the sentence onto the lines and underline the verb. Don't forget to give the line numbers!
Jetzt bist du dran – schau dir den Text noch einmal an und finde mindestens einen weiteren Satz mit einem Verb im Passiv – oder vielleicht schaffst du sogar zwei? Schreibe den Satz auf die Linien und unterstreiche das Verb. Vergiss die Zeilenangabe nicht!

4. ____

____

____ (line[s] ____________).

Sebastian Beckmann, Bill Lowenburg, Carina Welsch · Englisch-Krimi 7/8 | 978-3-589-16754-8 | Illustration Lupe: shutterstock/Sonya illustration; Hintergrund: shutterstock/Tobias Steinert

5. ______________________________

____

______________________________ (line[s] ________).

c) Think about it!

Have a look at the verbs from a) and b). Then fill in the different parts we need to form the passive of verbs into the boxes below. *Schau dir die Verben aus a) und b) genauer an. Schreibe dann die verschiedenen Teile, die wir für das Passiv eines Verbes brauchen, in die Kästchen.*

To make a verb passive, we need:

	+	________ (regular verbs) ________ (irregular verbs) ▷ ________ (expert word)

1. You often use the passive to give statistics or facts.
   2.500 cars were bought in Paris yesterday.
2. You do not use the passive to give personal or informal information.
   My brother bought a car. NOT: ~~A car was bought by my brother.~~
3. Not every sentence in the active can be put in the passive.
   Many French people live in Saarbrücken. ▷ *no passive*

B.2 Let's be active and passive!

a) Let's be passive!

Here are some sentences with active verbs. Rewrite them:

1. Use the passive. 2. Use the same tense as in the original.

Unten findest du einige Sätze, die aktive Formen verwenden. Schreibe diese ins Passiv um und behalte dabei die ursprüngliche Zeitform bei.

1. Mr. Irving called Detective Debs. ______________________________
2. Someone has stolen the prize horse. ______________________________
3. He introduced Debs to Billy Barnes. ______________________________
4. Mr. Barnes has trained the horses for 25 years. ______________________________

   ____
5. Extra: Within days, people would recognize SuperChamp. ______________________________

   ____

Sebastian Beckmann, Bill Lowenburg, Carina Welsch · Englisch-Krimi 7/8 | 978-3-589-16754-8 | Illustration Lupe: shutterstock/Sonya illustration; Hintergrund: shutterstock/Tobias Steinert

b) Let's be active!

Here are some sentences with passive verbs. Rewrite them: 1. Use the active. 2. Use the same tense as in the original.

Unten findest du einige Sätze, die passive Formen verwenden. Schreibe diese ins Aktiv um und behalte dabei die ursprüngliche Zeitform bei.

1. The gag was pulled from Mrs. Barnes' mouth by Debs.

____

____

2. Furniture was overturned in a fight by someone.

____

____

3. The lights were turned back down by Debs.

____

____

4. She was not taken seriously by many people.

____

____

5. Detective Debs was shown to the paddock by a very pretty young woman.

____

____

C BEYOND – CHOOSE ONE!

C.1 Asking Detective Debs

Imagine you are a reporter for a local newspaper. You are interviewing Detective Debs about the disappearance of SuperChamp. Write a short dialogue between the two people. You have to use at least three sentences in the passive.

Stell dir vor, du arbeitest für eine Lokalzeitung. Führe ein Interview mit Detective Debs über das Verschwinden von SuperChamp. Du musst mindestens drei Sätze im Passiv verwenden.

You can start like this:

Reporter: Hello, Detective Debs. Tell us something about SuperChamp's disappearance. What happened?

Debs: Hello! SuperChamp was kidnapped, but luckily, I was able to help the owner, Mr. Irving.

Reporter: Ok let's start at the beginning... Who called you in the first place?

Debs: I ...

Sebastian Beckmann, Bill Lowenburg, Carina Welsch · Englisch-Krimi 7/8 | 978-3-589-16754-8 | Illustration Lupe: shutterstock/Sonya illustration; Hintergrund: shutterstock/Tobias Steinert

C.2 A Letter

After Detective Debs solves the case and Bill Barnes is taken to the police station, he writes a letter to Mr. Irving in which he explains everything he did. Imagine you are Bill and write the letter from his perspective. You have to use at least three sentences in the passive.

Nachdem Detective Debs den Fall gelöst hat und Bill Barnes zur Polizeiinspektion mitgenommen worden ist, schreibt er einen Brief an Mr. Irving, in dem er erklärt, was er getan hat und seine Gründe darlegt. Stell dir vor, du bist Bill und schreibst den Brief. Verwende mindestens drei Verben im Passiv.

Start like this: Dear Mr. Irving, …

(to) work hard • (to) train the horses • (to) earn a lot of money • (to) earn little money • bad payment • (to) be angry

Sebastian Beckmann, Bill Lowenburg, Carina Welsch · Englisch-Krimi 7/8 | 978-3-589-16754-8 | Illustration Lupe: shutterstock/Sonya illustration; Hintergrund: shutterstock/Tobias Steinert

TOO GOOD TO BE TRUE

Johan Bopp was a very short man. He was also very old, 91. But he didn't feel old. Boppy, as his friends called him, measured 150 cm from his toes to the top of his bald head.[1] Mr. Bopp was well-educated, highly intelligent, and fluent in six languages. He owned several successful businesses, including the Bopp Shop Detective Agency. The sign outside the Bopp Shop said:

One Stop Shopping for Detective Work
Specialties Include:
Murder, Mayhem[2], Missing Persons,
and Miscellaneous Mischief[3]
Reasonable Rates[4]. Inquire Within[5]

On this particular morning, a Thursday, Bopp was sitting behind his desk enjoying his fifth cup of coffee while chatting with his assistant, Lisa Lott. Lisa was only fluent in five languages, but she made up for it in other ways. Lisa was 188 cm tall and was an international powerlifting[6] champion. She was also the Women's World Karate Champion, who fought under the name of Suzy Sweet. She had an undefeated record.[7]

A desperate-looking middle-aged man came staggering into the office from the street. He was dressed in a new and obviously expensive suit, but the suit was dirty and slashed[8] in many places. The man had a split lower lip[9] and a small trickle of blood running from his nose.

"Are you Bopp?" asked the man. He was out of breath.

"I am," replied Bopp. "You look like you could use a cup of coffee."

"That's for sure," said the man as he fell into the chair in front of Bopp's desk. "In fact, I could use something a bit stronger. Do you have any whiskey?"

"You are in luck," replied Bopp. He poured the man a cup of coffee, then reached down into his desk drawer and pulled out a bottle of whiskey. He poured a large shot of it into the man's coffee and passed the cup over to him.

"I can't believe what just happened," the man said, raising the cup to his lips with a shaky hand.

"You look like you were in a fight," Bopp observed.

---

1 bald head: no hair on the head
2 mayhem (n): *schwere Körperverletzung*
3 miscellaneous mischief (n): *sonstige Missetaten*
4 reasonable Rates: The cost for the detective work is not very high.
5 inquire Within: Ask about the rates inside.
6 powerlifting (n): Kraftdreikampf (Kreuzheben, Kniebeuge, Bankdrücken)
7 undefeated record: No one ever won against Lisa.
8 (to) be slashed: (to) have cuts
9 split lower lip (n): *gespaltene untere Lippe*

Sebastian Beckmann, Bill Lowenburg, Carina Welsch · Englisch-Krimi 7/8 | 978-3-589-16754-8 | Illustration Lupe: shutterstock/Sonya illustration; Hintergrund: shutterstock/Tobias Steinert

"I was," the man replied. "With two men, who kidnapped my wife!"

Bopp studied the man. There was something familiar about him, but for the moment Bopp could not tell where he'd seen the fellow before.

"Have you gone to the police?"

"No!" shouted the man. "The police cannot be involved! The kidnappers said if I contacted the police, I would never see my wife again. They demand one million dollars for her release." A little more blood dripped from the man's nose.

"Where do they think you're going to get that kind of money?" asked Lisa as she studied the man.

"My name is Tomas Buck. You might have seen me on TV."

"Buck – the financial advisor!" Bopp said. "I knew you looked familiar!"

"You tell people how to invest their money," Lisa added. "The kidnappers chose your wife because they knew you are rich."

"Exactly," Buck replied. He began to cry a little. "Because of who I am, I hope the bank will give me the money to pay the kidnappers."

"It so happens," said Bopp, "that I'm Chairman of the Board[10] at the bank! I will take care of it myself. In fact, I'll personally deliver the money when the kidnappers contact us."

"That's incredible, Mr. Bopp. I can't believe how kind you are!"

"Well, we always like to see justice[11] done, don't we Lisa?" He gave Lisa a little wink.

"Indeed," Lisa replied, winking back. "Would you like some more coffee, Mr. Buck?"

"Yes, please. This is very good whiskey, Mr. Bopp. Won't you join me?"

"Never touch the stuff," replied Bopp. "Now tell me exactly what happened."

"Okay," Buck began. "Two men with knives attacked my wife and me on the street. As you can see, we fought and fought! It was horrible! They pulled my wife into a car and drove off – to the West – leaving me with a ransom note[12]."

"What did the men look like?"

"They were short and strong, with dark hair and beards."

"Very good," said Bopp. "Did you notice any details about the car?"

"Yes! It was a black car with a green license plates!"

"Excellent," said Lisa. "That's very helpful."

Bopp then asked whether there had been any witnesses.

"Yes, thank God there were! Three people wrote down their names and telephone numbers for me."

He handed Lisa a crumpled piece of paper.

"How fortunate," Bopp said. "I'd say this case is well on the way to being solved."

"What's our next step?" asked Buck.

"Let me interview the witnesses," Bopp replied. "You go get yourself cleaned up, Mr. Buck. We'll be in touch by this evening."

---

10 Chairman of the Board (n.): Bopp is also one of the bosses at the bank.
11 justice (n): *die Gerechtigkeit*
12 ransom note (n): *die Lösegeldforderung*

"I don't know how to thank you, Mr. Bopp," said Buck. He looked much more optimistic than when he had come into the office.

As soon as Buck left, Bopp poured[13] himself a fresh cup of coffee. He looked at Lisa. She was laughing.

"Interesting story, eh, Boppy?"

"Very interesting," replied Bopp. "Of course, he's lying."

"One of the worst liars we've ever seen," laughed Lisa. "And we've seen a lot of them."

"Follow him. I'm going to talk to the so-called witnesses. I'll call you later."

"Ok, Chief."

Lisa left to follow Buck and Bopp called the witnesses. All three gave exactly the same story, right down to the smallest details: two short, strong men with dark hair and beards, a small black car with green license plates, heading West. This confirmed everything Bopp had believed so far.

Just as Bopp reached for the telephone, it rang. It was Lisa.

"Ok, Boss, it's just what we thought. I've got them under observation.[14] Shall I arrest them?"

"Go ahead, if you're in the mood. I'll bring the police."

"Great," said Lisa. "Have them bring the transport van. I just cleaned my car and don't want those dirty criminals in it. Do you need directions?"

"No, don't bother. I know where to find you," said Bopp. "See you soon." Then he called the police.

What Lisa was observing from her hiding place was Buck, his wife, and their five partners sitting around a table playing cards, drinking whiskey, and smoking cigarettes. They were having a great time.

When Bopp and the police entered the abandoned warehouse[15] on the waterfront, this is what they saw: Buck, his wife, and the three witnesses were handcuffed[16] to chairs with tape over their mouths. The two kidnappers, however, were in a different condition. One had been stuffed upside down into an open barrel[17] and his legs were kicking wildly. The other was lying in the corner, groaning.[18] He had good reason to groan, as he was suffering from a broken jaw,[19] a concussion, three broken ribs, and a broken shoulder. Additionally, five of his teeth were missing and lay scattered on the floor beside him.

"My, my, my, Lisa," said Bopp as he and the police officers studied the scene. "What a shame."

"Sorry, Boss, but the boys here tried to fight with me when I arrested them. I had to take their knives away."

The men Lisa referred to as "the boys," were not short and strong with dark hair and beards, but were in fact tall and blonde.

"So, Boppy," said the police Sergeant, "Please explain this to me. How did you know the whole thing was a fake from the beginning?"

"Very simple. To begin with, Mr. Buck's suit had been cut in many places, suggesting he'd been in a violent struggle. But he had not one scratch[20] or cut on his skin. Someone had carefully cut his suit with a knife.

---

13 (to) pour: (to) put coffee into a mug
14 observation (n): *die Beobachtung*
15 abandoned warehouse (n): *leerstehende Lagerhalle*
16 (to) be handcuffed: *in Handschellen sein*
17 barrel (n): *das Fass*
18 (to) groan: *stöhnen*
19 jaw (n): *der Kiefer*
20 scratch (n): *der Kratzer*

Sebastian Beckmann, Bill Lowenburg, Carina Welsch · Englisch-Krimi 7/8 | 978-3-589-16754-8 | Illustration Lupe: shutterstock/Sonya illustration; Hintergrund: shutterstock/Tobias Steinert

The bloody nose and lip were easily accomplished with makeup."

"Fascinating. Go on."

"Then, Mr. Buck's details about the kidnappers and their car matched ***exactly*** with the stories of the witnesses. Eye-witnesses are always inaccurate with details. They ***never*** get things right. All three witnesses agreed with Buck in every single detail! So obviously they were all following one story."

"But why?" wondered the Sergeant. "What's the point of it all? Buck is a very rich man. Why would he do this?"

"Maybe he's not really so rich. Let's ask him."

Bopp peeled the tape away from Buck's mouth.

"I might as well admit it," Buck explained. "I've lost all my money to gambling[21] and bad investments. I was down to my last thousand Euros."

"So you hired these idiots to act out a story, hoping for a fast million?"

"Yes. They were all I could get for my money."

Bopp replaced the tape on Buck's mouth. Now Mrs. Buck wanted to say something, so Bopp removed her tape.

"So what crime did we commit? No money was taken from the bank!"

"Good point, Mrs. Buck," said the Sergeant. "However, this white car here doesn't belong to you, it was reported stolen. We're also charging all of you with fraud and extortion.[22] Not to mention that your colleagues who attacked Lisa tried to kill her."

"And, finally," said Bopp, "I will make your husband pay for my detective services. He hired me to find you. And I did." He replaced the tape on Mrs. Buck's mouth before she could reply. The Sergeant was highly amused.

"Well done, Bopp," said the Sergeant. "But how did you know where to find them?"

"Quite simple," Bopp explained. "Their story said they drove West in a black car, so naturally they really drove East. To the East of the city is the waterfront, with all of the abandoned warehouses. Kidnappers always hide in abandoned warehouses. I just had to look for the one with the ***white*** car parked outside."

"Amazing," said the Sergeant, shaking his head. "You make it look easy, Boppy."

"It is," replied Bopp. "At my age, there aren't too many surprises. I'll leave it to you to clean up here, Sergeant. Lisa and I are going for some coffee."

21 gambling (n): *das Glücksspiel*

22 fraud and extortion (n): *Betrug und Erpressung*

TOO GOOD TO BE TRUE – ACTIVITIES

A CONTENT

A.1 Are you on the right track?

Read the following statements and for each of them, decide if it is true or false. Correct the false statements.

Can you find the line of the text for each of the statements?

Lies dir die folgenden Sätze durch und entscheide, ob sie richtig oder falsch sind. Verbessere die falschen Aussagen.

Kannst du für die Sätze die Textstellen finden, an denen die Informationen stehen?

1. Boppy is the clever owner of several successful businesses and is fluent in seven languages.

   ☐ True ☐ False: ____________________

2. He is very old but he does not feel so.

   ☐ True ☐ False: ____________________

3. Boppy's assistant is called Lisa Lott and she is a weak person.

   ☐ True ☐ False: ____________________

4. Mister Buck is a lawyer whose wife was kidnapped.

   ☐ True ☐ False: ____________________

5. Lisa follows Mister Buck and Boppy interviews the witnesses who all give the same story.

   ☐ True ☐ False: ____________________

6. When Boppy and the police arrived at the warehouse, they found Mister Buck, his wife and the three witnesses handcuffed and with tape over their mouths.

   ☐ True ☐ False: ____________________

7. As no money was taken from the bank, Mister Buck isn't in trouble and can go home.

   ☐ True ☐ False: ____________________

A.2 Too good to be true?

a) How did Boppy know where to find Lisa, Mister Buck and the others?

Woher hat Boppy gewusst, wo er Lisa, Mister Buck und die anderen finden kann?

____

____

____

____

b) Explain the title of the story. What is too good to be true? Why?

Erkläre den Titel der Geschichte. Was ist „zu schön, um wahr zu sein"? Warum?

____

____

____

____

B LANGUAGE

B.1 People, get ready!

Read the following information on countable and uncountable nouns.

Lies dir die folgenden Informationen über zählbare und unzählbare Nomen durch.

Countable nouns have singular and plural forms, most nouns are countable.

a car → two cars   one detective → two detectives

a bottle → two bottles

Some nouns are **uncountable**, they only have one form.

blood   police   money   water   information

You cannot use *a/an*, or *numbers* with an uncountable noun.

a blood   two polices   a money   three water   an information

Often, uncountable nouns refer to things (bread, chocolate, butter, milk, soap) and abstract ideas or emotions (grammar, love, hate, education, knowledge). Often, *some* is used with uncountable nouns: some money, some water, some information.

Sebastian Beckmann, Bill Lowenburg, Carina Welsch · Englisch-Krimi 7/8 | 978-3-589-16754-8 | Illustration Lupe: shutterstock/Sonya illustration; Hintergrund: shutterstock/Tobias Steinert

B.2 Easy peasy lemon squeezy!

Write down the plural forms of the following nouns if they are countable. If they are uncountable, note UC.

Schreibe die Pluralformen der folgenden Nomen auf, falls diese existieren. Falls das nicht der Fall ist, notiere UC.

a. child ____________________ d. car ____________________

b. information ____________________ e. water ____________________

c. piece ____________________ f. coffee ____________________

B.3 Go and find them!

a. Read the following text about the beginning of the story.

Lies den folgenden Text über den Anfang der Geschichte.

"TOO GOOD TO BE TRUE" is a story about Johan Bopp, called Boppy, who runs a detective agency and who is able to speak six languages. One Thursday morning, a man came in, introduced himself as Tomas Buck, and explained that his wife had been kidnapped in front of his eyes. Boppy and his assistant Lisa could see that Buck had a dirty suit, a split lower lip, and a small trickle of blood running from his nose. Buck explained that the police cannot be involved because then he would never see his wife again. Lisa said that the kidnappers chose his wife in order to get a lot of money because they knew that he was rich.

b. Underline all nouns in the text.

Unterstreiche alle Nomen im Text.

c. In the table below, fill in the nouns from b) in the correct column depending on whether they are used as countable or uncountable nouns.

Fülle die Nomen aus b) in die Tabelle ein, je nachdem, ob sie zählbar oder unzählbar sind.

Countable	Uncountable

Sebastian Beckmann, Bill Lowenburg, Carina Welsch · Englisch-Krimi 7/8 | 978-3-589-16754-8 | Illustration Lupe: shutterstock/Sonya illustration; Hintergrund: shutterstock/Tobias Steinert

B.4 Practice!

Put the expressions below in the correct box.

Ordne die Begriffe unten den beiden Kategorien links zu.

Expressions which go with countable nouns
Expressions which go with uncountable nouns

How much …?   How many …?   these   a little   much   a few   this   many   a lot of

B.5 Let's take some action!

Fill in the gaps using one of the following: many/much/a lot of/a few/a little.

Fülle die Lücken mit einem der folgenden Wörter: many/much/a lot of/a few/little.

1. Boppy has solved ______________ cases in the last 70 years.
2. Tomas likes to drink ______________ of whiskey.
3. Boppy enjoys drinking ______________ coffee.
4. ______________ people trust the Bopp Shop Detective Agency.
5. It turns out that Tomas only has ______________ money.
6. Lisa Lott can speak ______________ languages.
7. ______________ hours later, Boppy and Lisa are able to solve the case.
8. ______________ of questions are asked at the end.
9. Lisa and Boppy do not need ______________ time to find out that Tomas is not honest with them.

Sebastian Beckmann, Bill Lowenburg, Carina Welsch · Englisch-Krimi 7/8 | 978-3-589-16754-8 | Illustration Lupe: shutterstock/Sonya illustration; Hintergrund: shutterstock/Tobias Steinert

C BEYOND – CHOOSE ONE!

C.1 Mister Buck's Diary

Imagine you are Mister Buck and you come home at the end of this day. From his point of view, write a diary entry in which you tell the diary about the plan, the visit at Boppy's agency, Lisa coming to the warehouse and how everything ended. Make sure to include his thoughts and feelings.

Stell dir vor, du bist Mister Buck, und du kommst am Ende dieses Tages nach Hause. Schreibe einen Tagebucheintrag aus seiner Perspektive, in dem du deinem Tagebuch von dem Plan, dem Besuch in Boppys Büro, Lisas Ankunft bei der Lagerhalle erzählst und davon, wie alles geendet ist. Achte dabei darauf, auch seine Gedanken und Gefühle miteinzubeziehen.

Start like this:

Dear diary, ____________________

(to) run out of money • (to) make a plan • (to) mislead someone • (to) stick to a story • accomplice (Komplize) • (to) discover the truth • consequences

Sebastian Beckmann, Bill Lowenburg, Carina Welsch · Englisch-Krimi 7/8 | 978-3-589-16754-8 | Illustration Lupe: shutterstock/Sonya illustration; Hintergrund: shutterstock/Tobias Steinert

C.2 Lisa and the Buck story

Put yourself in Lisa's shoes. Re-read the story and take notes on what she did in the different scenes of the story. Imagine Lisa meets a friend after work and tells the story from her point of view.

Versetze dich in Lisa. Lies die Geschichte noch einmal und mache dir Notizen dazu, was sie in den verschiedenen Szenen der Geschichte gemacht hat. Stell dir vor, Lisa trifft nach der Arbeit an diesem Tag eine Freundin; erzähle die Geschichte aus ihrer Sicht.

Start like this:

Today was a crazy day. Just imagine, I was sitting in our office chatting to my boss when …

(to) have a client • (to) see through somebody [= jemanden durchschauen] • (to) make a plan • (to) call somebody to account for sth [= jemanden für etwas zur Rechenschaft ziehen]

Sebastian Beckmann, Bill Lowenburg, Carina Welsch · Englisch-Krimi 7/8 | 978-3-589-16754-8 | Illustration Lupe: shutterstock/Sonya illustration; Hintergrund: shutterstock/Tobias Steinert

THE GREAT PIZZA ROBBERIES[1]

Joe's Pizza King was located near a rough part of the city. Many crimes took place in the neighborhood. But Joe's was very successful because they had the best pizza and the most reliable delivery team. The pizza shop also stayed open late. The delivery men and women were required to use their own car and they were not paid well. They did not even receive free pizza or a discount. Joe, their boss, was a nice guy, but he was kind of a cheapskate.

William, the newest deliveryman, had been hired several weeks earlier and he was doing a great job. William had a big old car and seemed to know his way around all parts of the city. He soon became Joe's best deliveryman and Joe was happy, because his business was growing.

Then one Thursday night, William was robbed while making a delivery. It was an unusual robbery, for two reasons. First, it took place on a busy street. Eyewitnesses[1] reported that just as William got out of his car with the pizza, a teenage boy ran up, pointed a pistol, and ran off with the pizza. Second, no money was taken, just the pizza!

A few weeks later on a Thursday night, a similar thing happened near a small shopping center. This time the robber was a teenage girl. She pulled out a gun, said a few words to William, and ran off with two pizzas, but no cash.

1 An eyewitness is someone who sees a crime.

 | Sebastian Beckmann, Bill Lowenburg, Carina Welsch · Englisch-Krimi 7/8 | 978-3-589-16754-8 |
Illustration: o.: Dorina Tessmann; Lupe: shutterstock/Sonya illustration; Hintergrund: shutterstock/Tobias Steinert

Of course, Joe was concerned for both his delivery team and for his business. He didn't want any of his employees to get hurt. He also knew that if the robberies continued, customers would soon stop ordering. The police were investigating, but to be honest, they weren't working very hard on the case. One day, Joe went to the police station to get an update from Sergeant Kratz. Kratz was eating a sandwich that did not look very appetizing.

"A pizza?" said Kratz. "I'm supposed to get excited about a missing pizza? I'm dealing with bank robberies, drug deals, and shootings, and you want me to assign[2] officers to investigate a pizza? I am not going to waste my time with a pizza!"

"I understand," replied Joe. "Of course, if your officers have any spare time, they are welcome to stop by the shop for a free slice or two and I can update them."

"Hmm," said Kratz. "I'll have a look into this myself. I'll see you around lunchtime on Friday."

A month went by. No new robberies. Sergeant Kratz stopped by the shop two or three times a week and tried every different kind of pizza offered on the menu. He appeared to be gaining weight. However, there was no new information on the case.

Then one Thursday night, William got robbed again, this time near a busy pharmacy. According to witnesses, the robber was a woman who appeared to be about William's age.

"I can't understand it," Joe exclaimed when William returned to the shop. "None of the other delivery people get robbed, just you! And always on a Thursday night! Why is that?"

"Maybe it's because I deliver to the bad part of town," William replied.

"That's possible," said Joe. "But why doesn't the thief take your money, too?"

"I have no explanation," answered William.

Since the police were no help, Joe decided to take matters into his own hands. He began following William on his deliveries. He stayed a safe distance behind and used several different cars so William would not catch on. Every evening the following week, Joe followed William. He could easily see why William was his number one deliveryman. He was fast, efficient, and friendly to the customers.

Monday evening, no problem. Tuesday, the same. Wednesday, the same again. Late on Thursday evening, however, in the bad part of town, Joe observed through binoculars[3] as William was robbed. It was the teenage girl once again. Following the robbery, William drove his big old car back toward the pizza shop.

Instead of following William, Joe trailed[4] the robber at a safe distance. She appeared to be a nice girl, perhaps sixteen years old. Anyone encountering[5] her would think she had just bought a pizza instead of robbing someone at gunpoint[6]. Joe was baffled.

As the girl continued, the neighborhood became rougher and rougher. Many of the buildings were dark and abandoned[7]. There were few streetlights. Finally, the girl entered one of the buildings. It too was dark, except for a flicker of light from a window on the second floor. Joe parked his car nearby, shut off the engine, and observed. For over an hour, no one else passed on the street.

---

2 (to) assign: (to) give someone a job / something to take care of
3 binoculars (n and plural): *das Fernglas*
4 (to) trail: (to) follow
5 (to) encounter: (to) meet / (to) see
6 (to) rob someone at gunpoint: (to) rob someone with a gun
7 (to) abandon: (to) leave someone / something alone

Sebastian Beckmann, Bill Lowenburg, Carina Welsch · Englisch-Krimi 7/8 | 978-3-589-16754-8 | Illustration Lupe: shutterstock/Sonya illustration; Hintergrund: shutterstock/Tobias Steinert

Just as Joe was getting ready to go back to the shop, a car pulled up to the building with its headlights[8] off. Seeing a man get out of the car, Joe turned on his headlights. It was William! Joe started his car and sped over to the building.

"What is the meaning of this?" Joe shouted from his car as he stopped.

"So, you've discovered my secret," William replied.

"Secret?"

"We're homeless," William explained. My family and I have been living in this abandoned building for two months now. Before that, we lived in my car."

"Why didn't you tell me?" Joe asked.

"I was ashamed," William replied. "I want to work and earn money, but you pay so little that some weeks we can't make it to Friday. There are too many mouths to feed now with the baby."

"There's a baby?"

"Yes, she's six months old. Come in and see her and meet my family."

Joe followed William up the dark stairs to the second floor, where he was introduced to William's wife, his teenage son and daughter, and little Emma. They were eating the pizza in a sparsely furnished room[9] lit by candles. On the table next to the pizza box, Joe saw the pistol. It was a cheap plastic toy.

"Soon we must move," William's wife said. "The summer is ending and it's getting colder. We can't make a fire here or we'll be discovered."

Joe's head was spinning as he tried to understand everything that had happened.

"Why did you fake the robberies in front of witnesses?" Joe asked.

"So you wouldn't think I was making it up[10]," William replied.

"And why did you take no money? That's what I really can't understand."

"Ah, that's the key," William explained. "Then the police would have worked harder. We only needed to make it to Friday, when I got paid."

"Now I'm the one who feels ashamed – if only I had known!" said Joe. "I'm giving you a raise[11] and I also have a place for you to live."

"A home?"

"Well, a nice flat, anyway. Next month I'm opening Joe's Pizza King II on the other side of town. You and your wife can manage it and everyone can live upstairs. Your teens can make deliveries. Everyone except little Emma will have a job."

"Thank you," said William. "I'll pay you back for those pizzas."

---

8 headlights (n and plural): lights at the front of a car
9 sparsely furnished room: a room with almost no furniture (table, chairs, bed)
10 (to) make something up: (to) fake
11 raise (n): *die Gehaltserhöhung*

Sebastian Beckmann, Bill Lowenburg, Carina Welsch · Englisch-Krimi 7/8 | 978-3-589-16754-8 | Illustration Lupe: shutterstock/Sonya illustration; Hintergrund: shutterstock/Tobias Steinert

THE GREAT PIZZA ROBBERIES - BASIC LEVEL

A LANGUAGE

A.1 What happened when?

Take a look at the following events from the story and put them into the correct order.

Lies dir die Sätze durch und bringe sie in die richtige Reihenfolge.

a) Joe followed William.
b) The police started an investigation.
c) William was robbed by teenage girl.
d) Joe found out about the true nature of the robbery.
e) Sergeant Kratz ate a lot of pizza but did not find out any new information.
f) William was robbed on a busy street. The robber took nothing but the pizza.

1	2	3	4	5	6

A.2 A robbery?

a) Why do the robbers only take the pizza, but not the money?
Warum stehlen die Diebe immer nur die Pizza, nicht aber das Geld?

____

____

____

b) Why do the robberies always take place on a Thursday?
Warum finden die Diebstähle immer donnerstags statt?

____

____

____

B LANGUAGE

B.1 Off you go!

Let's see what you can remember! Fill in the table with the missing verbs in their correct forms.

Schauen wir, woran du dich erinnerst! Fülle die fehlenden Verben in ihrer richtigen Zeit in die Lücken der Tabelle.

Statements

1.	"They ___are___ (to be) welcome to stop by the shop for a slice of pizza." ***(simple present)***	→	He said that they ___were___ welcome to stop by the shop for a slice of pizza. ***(simple past)***
2.	"I ____________ with (to deal with) bank robberies." ***(simple present progressive)***	→	Kratz said that he ____________ with bank robberies. ***(simple past progressive)***
3.	"A teenage boy ____________ and ____________ (to run up/to point) a pistol." ***(simple past)***	→	He said that a teenage boy ____________ and ____________ a pistol. ***(past perfect)***
4.	"You ____________ (to discover) my secret." ***(present perfect)***	→	William said that he ____________ his secret. ***(past perfect)***
5.	"If only I ____________ (to know)." ***(past perfect)***	→	He said that if only he ____________. ***(past perfect)***
6.	"I ____________________ my time with a pizza!" (to not waste) ***(going to-future)***	→	Kratz said that he ____________ ____________ his time for a pizza. ***(was/were + not going to)***
7.	"I ____________ (to have a look) into this myself and ____________ (to see) you on Friday." ***(will-future)***	→	He said that he ____________ ____________ into that himself and ____________ him on Friday. ***(would/conditional)***

Need some help? The following lines can help you.

Brauchst du Hilfe? Die folgenden Zeilenangaben helfen dir.

line 26, line 21, lines 11, line 55, line 75, line 22–23, lines 26

Sebastian Beckmann, Bill Lowenburg, Carina Welsch · Englisch-Krimi 7/8 | 978-3-589-16754-8 | Illustration Lupe: shutterstock/Sonya illustration; Hintergrund: shutterstock/Tobias Steinert

Questions

Find the following two questions in the text, then have a look at how they are changed into reported speech.

Finde die folgenden beiden Fragen im Text und schau dir dann an, wie sie in der indirekten Rede verändert werden.

Questions with question words “____________________ ____________________?”	→	Joe asked *why* William **hadn't told** him about his situation.
Yes/No Questions “____________________ ____________________?”	→	Joe asked *if/whether* there **was** a baby.

B.2 Track them down!

It's time for you to use the knowledge you gained so far and take matters in your own hands – just as Joe does! Have a look at the highlighted verbs in the text and change the direct statements from the text into reported/indirect statements. Remember to include all necessary changes.

Es ist an der Zeit, das Wissen, das du bisher gewonnen hast, zu nutzen und die Dinge in deine Hand zu nehmen – so, wie Joe. Schau dir die markierten Verben im Text an und wandle die Sätze von der direkten Rede in die indirekte Rede um. Denke dabei daran, alle notwendigen Änderungen vorzunehmen.

1. line 24–25: *Joe said that* ____________________

____________________.

2. line 32–33: *Joe remarked that* ____________________.

He said that ____________________.

3. line 34: *William replied that maybe* ____________________.

4. line 35: *Joe said that* ____________________. He asked

____________________.

5. line 36: *William answered that* ____________________

____________________.

6. line 54: *Joe asked* ____________________.

Sebastian Beckmann, Bill Lowenburg, Carina Welsch · Englisch-Krimi 7/8 | 978-3-589-16754-8 | Illustration Lupe: shutterstock/Sonya illustration; Hintergrund: shutterstock/Tobias Steinert

7. line 55: *William replied that Joe* ______________________________

______________________________.

8. line 60: *William replied that* ______________________________ and that

______________________________ to Friday.

You want some more? Go ahead!

9. line 67: *William's wife said that* ______________________________

______________________________.

10. line 70: *Joe asked* ______________________________

______________________________.

B.3 The other way around

Rewrite the following sentences and turn them into direct speech.
Tip: There is help in the text if you need it.
Schreibe die folgenden Sätze in direkte Rede um. Tipp: Du findest Hilfen zu den Sätzen im Text.

1. Kratz asked if he was supposed to get excited about a missing pizza.

Kratz: "Am I ______________________________?"

2. Joe said the he couldn't understand what was going on.

Joe: "______________________________."

3. William emphasized that he delivered to the bad part of town.

William: "______________________________."

4. William saw Joe and said to his boss that he had discovered William's secret.

William: "______________________________."

5. William complained that he and his family couldn't make it to Friday.

William: "______________________________."

Sebastian Beckmann, Bill Lowenburg, Carina Welsch · Englisch-Krimi 7/8 | 978-3-589-16754-8 | Illustration Lupe: shutterstock/Sonya illustration; Hintergrund: shutterstock/Tobias Steinert

C BEYOND – CHOOSE ONE!

C.1 "Welcome to your News Report – are you ready for the latest news?"

Imagine you are a journalist and you heard about the events at Joe's Pizza King. Of course, you want to tell the world about the story. Write a newspaper article. Remember you need a catchy headline to get the reader interested. Use at least 3 reported speech constructions.

Stell dir vor, du bist ein Journalist und hast von den Ereignissen bei Joe's Pizza King gehört. Natürlich willst du der Welt berichten, was passiert ist. Schreibe einen Zeitungsartikel. Denke daran, eine griffige Überschrift zu finden, die den Lesern Lust macht, weiterzulesen. Verwende mindestens 3 Sätze in der indirekten Rede.

Your Headline:

____

Your Article:

____

____

____

____

____

____

____

____

____

____

____

____

(to) report • (to) state • (to) ask •
thief • hunger • (to) starve (hungern) • starving family • (to) survive •
not what it seemed • (to) support

Sebastian Beckmann, Bill Lowenburg, Carina Welsch · Englisch-Krimi 7/8 | 978-3-589-16754-8 | Illustration Lupe: shutterstock/Sonya illustration; Hintergrund: shutterstock/Tobias Steinert

C.2 Joe's Witness Report

Joe from *Joe's Pizza King* has to give a witness statement. From his point of view, tell the police officer about William, the pizza robberies and the things he finds out in the end. Also, include what Joe wants the police to do in the case: should William be punished? Why? Why not?

Joe von Joe's Pizza King soll eine Zeugenaussage zu den Ereignissen machen. Erzähle dem Polizisten – aus Joes Blickwinkel – von William, den Pizzadiebstählen und davon, was er herausgefunden hat. Ende damit, was Joe der Polizei vorschlägt, in seinem Fall zu tun. Sollte William bestraft werden? Warum? Warum nicht?

Start like this:

Police officer: "So tell me what happened – from the very beginning. You said that there had been pizza robberies at your Pizza King …"

Joe: "Well …"

"

(to) report • (to) state • (to) ask •
thief • every Thursday • deliveryman • hunger • (to) starve (hungern) •
starving family • (to) survive • not what it seemed •
(to) support • duty (Pflicht) to help • (to) learn a lesson

Sebastian Beckmann, Bill Lowenburg, Carina Welsch • Englisch-Krimi 7/8 | 978-3-589-16754-8 | Illustration Lupe: shutterstock/Sonya illustration; Hintergrund: shutterstock/Tobias Steinert

THE GREAT PIZZA ROBBERIES – ADVANCED LEVEL

A LANGUAGE

A.1 What happened when?

Take a look at the following events from the story and put them into the correct order.

Lies dir die Sätze durch und bringe sie in die richtige Reihenfolge.

a) Joe followed William.
b) The police started an investigation.
c) William was robbed by teenage girl.
d) Joe found out about the true nature of the robbery.
e) Sergeant Kratz ate a lot of pizza but did not find out any new information.
f) William was robbed on a busy street. The robber took nothing but the pizza.

1	2	3	4	5	6

A.2 A robbery?

a) Why do the robbers only take the pizza, but not the money?
Warum stehlen die Diebe immer nur die Pizza, nicht aber das Geld?

___

___

___

b) Why do the robberies always take place on a Thursday?
Warum finden die Diebstähle immer donnerstags statt?

___

___

___

B LANGUAGE

B.1 Off you go!

Let's see what you can remember! Fill in the table with the missing verbs in their correct forms.

Schauen wir, woran du dich erinnerst! Fülle die fehlenden Verben in ihrer richtigen Zeit in die Lücken der Tabelle.

Statements

1.	"They ___________ (to be) welcome to stop by the shop for a slice of pizza." ***(simple present)***	→	He said that they ___________ welcome to stop by the shop for a slice of pizza. ***(simple past)***
2.	"I ___________ with (to deal with) bank robberies." ***(simple present progressive)***	→	Kratz said that he ___________ with bank robberies. ***(simple past progressive)***
3.	"A teenage boy ___________ and ___________ (to run up/to point) a pistol." ***(simple past)***	→	He said that a teenage boy ___________ and ___________ a pistol. ***(past perfect)***
4.	"You ___________ (to discover) my secret." ***(present perfect)***	→	William said that he ___________ his secret. ***(past perfect)***
5.	"If only I ___________ (to know)." ***(past perfect)***	→	He said that if only he ___________. ***(past perfect)***
6.	"I ___________________ my time with a pizza!" (to not waste) ***(going to-future)***	→	Kratz said that he ___________ ___________ his time for a pizza. ***(was/were + not going to)***
7.	"I ___________ (to have a look) into this myself and ___________ (to see) you on Friday." ***(will-future)***	→	He said that he ___________ ___________ into that himself and ___________ him on Friday. ***(would/conditional)***

Sebastian Beckmann, Bill Lowenburg, Carina Welsch · Englisch-Krimi 7/8 | 978-3-589-16754-8 | Illustration Lupe: shutterstock/Sonya illustration; Hintergrund: shutterstock/Tobias Steinert

Questions

Find the following two questions in the text, then have a look at how they are changed into reported speech.

Finde die folgenden beiden Fragen im Text und schau dir dann an, wie sie in der indirekten Rede verändert werden.

Questions with question words "____________________ ____________________?"	→	Joe asked *why* William **hadn't told** him about his situation.
Yes/No Questions "____________________ ____________________?"	→	Joe asked *if/whether* there **was** a baby.

B.2 Track them down!

It's time for you to use the knowledge you gained so far and take matters in your own hands – just as Joe does! Have a look at the highlighted verbs in the text and change the direct statements from the text into reported/indirect statements. Remember to include all necessary changes.

Es ist an der Zeit, das Wissen, das du bisher gewonnen hast, zu nutzen und die Dinge in Deine Hand zu nehmen – so, wie Joe. Schau dir die markierten Verben im Text an und wandle die Sätze von der direkten Rede in die indirekte Rede um. Denke dabei daran, alle notwendigen Änderungen vorzunehmen.

1. line 24–25: *Joe said that* ____________________

____________________.

2. line 32–33: *Joe remarked that* ____________________.

He said that ____________________.

3. line 34: *William replied that maybe* ____________________.

4. line 35: *Joe said that* ____________________. He asked

____________________.

5. line 36: *William answered that* ____________________

____________________.

6. line 54: *Joe asked* ____________________.

Sebastian Beckmann, Bill Lowenburg, Carina Welsch · Englisch-Krimi 7/8 | 978-3-589-16754-8 | Illustration Lupe: shutterstock/Sonya illustration; Hintergrund: shutterstock/Tobias Steinert

7. line 55: *William replied that Joe* ______________________________

____.

8. line 60: *William replied that* ______________________________ and that

____ to Friday.

You want some more? Go ahead!

9. line 67: *William's wife said that* ______________________________

____.

10. line 70: *Joe asked* ______________________________

____.

B.3 The other way around

Rewrite the following sentences and turn them into direct speech.

Schreibe die folgenden Sätze in direkte Rede um.

1. Kratz asked if he was supposed to get excited about a missing pizza.

Kratz: "Am I ______________________________?"

2. Joe said the he couldn't understand what was going on.

Joe: "______________________________."

3. William emphasized that he delivered to the bad part of town.

William: "______________________________."

4. William saw Joe and said to his boss that he had discovered William's secret.

William: "______________________________."

5. William complained that he and his family couldn't make it to Friday.

William: "______________________________."

Sebastian Beckmann, Bill Lowenburg, Carina Welsch • Englisch-Krimi 7/8 | 978-3-589-16754-8 | Illustration Lupe: shutterstock/Sonya illustration; Hintergrund: shutterstock/Tobias Steinert

C BEYOND – CHOOSE ONE!

C.1 "Welcome to your News Report – are you ready for the latest news?"

Imagine you are a journalist and you heard about the events at Joe's Pizza King.
Of course, you want to tell the world about the story.
Write a newspaper article. Remember you need a catchy headline to get the reader interested. Use at least 3 reported speech constructions.

Stell dir vor, du bist ein Journalist und hast von den Ereignissen bei Joes Pizza King gehört.
Natürlich willst du der Welt berichten, was passiert ist.
Schreibe einen Zeitungsartikel. Denke daran, eine griffige Überschrift zu finden, die den Lesern Lust macht, weiterzulesen. Verwende mindestens 3 Sätze in der indirekten Rede.

Your Headline:

____

Your Article:

____

____

____

____

____

____

____

____

____

____

____

____

(to) report • (to) state • (to) ask •
thief • hunger • (to) starve (hungern) • starving family • (to) survive •
not what it seemed • (to) support ✿ Robin Hood

Sebastian Beckmann, Bill Lowenburg, Carina Welsch · Englisch-Krimi 7/8 | 978-3-589-16754-8 | Illustration Lupe: shutterstock/Sonya illustration; Hintergrund: shutterstock/Tobias Steinert

C.2 Joe's Witness Report

Joe from *Joe's Pizza King* has to give a witness statement. From his point of view, tell the police officer about William, the pizza robberies and the things he finds out in the end. Also, include what Joe wants the police to do in the case: should William be punished? Why? Why not?

Joe von Joe's Pizza King soll eine Zeugenaussage zu den Ereignissen machen. Erzähle dem Polizisten – aus Joes Blickwinkel – von William, den Pizzadiebstählen und davon, was er herausgefunden hat. Ende damit, was Joe der Polizei vorschlägt, in seinem Fall zu tun. Sollte William bestraft werden? Warum? Warum nicht?

Start like this:

Police officer: "So tell me what happened – from the very beginning. You said that there had been pizza robberies at your Pizza King …"

Joe: "Well …"

____

____

____

____

____

____

____

____

____

____

____

____"

(to) report • (to) state • (to) ask
thief • every Thursday • deliveryman • hunger • (to) starve (hungern) •
starving family • (to) survive • not what it seemed
(to) support • duty (Pflicht) to help • (to) learn a lesson • Robin Hood

Sebastian Beckmann, Bill Lowenburg, Carina Welsch · Englisch-Krimi 7/8 | 978-3-589-16754-8 | Illustration Lupe: shutterstock/Sonya illustration; Hintergrund: shutterstock/Tobias Steinert

IGOR THE BRAVE

IGOR THE BRAVE – A.1 Something is wrong here! Seite 8/12

1. Igor is called the Shy.
2. Igor is not small, he is a big dog and weighs 90 kg.
3. They are, but not inside.
4. She wants to go out with him (but Igor has to stay home).
5. It's not Mr., but Mrs. Trinkenschuh.

IGOR THE BRAVE – A.2 Igor the Brave, Robert the Shy – or the other way around? Seite 8/12

Igor is called the Brave at the beginning but is shy when it comes to Zsa-Zsa in the end, Robert says about himself that he is shy at the beginning, but he is brave in the end when he asks Suzy to go out with him.

IGOR THE BRAVE – B.1 It's a match! Seite 9

Basic Level

Type 1	If Robert asks Suzy, she will go out with him.	real, möglich, erfüllbar
Type 2	If Robert asked Suzy, she would go out with him.	unwahrscheinlich
Type 3	If Robert had asked Suzy, she would have gone out with him.	unmöglich, nicht mehr erfüllbar

Seite 12

Advanced Level

Type 1	If Robert asks Suzy, she will go out with him.	possible
Type 2	If Robert asked Suzy, she would go out with him.	unlikely or impossible
Type 3	If Robert had asked Suzy, she would have gone out with him.	impossible

IGOR THE BRAVE – B.2 The three ifs ... Seite 9/13

a) 1. If Robert was six inches taller, he would not be so shy.
   2. If we are hungry, we will eat a sandwich, too.
   3. If Robert hadn't taken so long with the drinks, he wouldn't have had problems with his sandwich.

b) 4. If you tell Igor to watch the table, he will do it even on bad days.
   5. If Robert had asked Suzy earlier, she would have said yes.
   6. If Zsa-Zsa wasn't so cute, Igor wouldn't cover his face with his paws.

IGOR THE BRAVE – B.3 What if? Seite 10/13

a) If Robert had not been too shy, he would have told Suzy that he has a crush on her.
b) If Robert had not gone to get his drink, Igor would not have had to guard the sandwich and the money.
c) If Robert had not taken such a long time to choose his drink, the sandwich and the money would have still been therel.
d) If Igor had guarded the table, Robert would not have been disappointed.
e) If the shop had not had a security camera, they would not have found out about Mrs. Trinkenschuh and Zsa-Zsa.

Sebastian Beckmann, Bill Lowenburg, Carina Welsch · Englisch-Krimi 7/8 | 978-3-589-16754-8 | Illustration Lupe: shutterstock/Sonya illustration; Hintergrund: shutterstock/Tobias Steinert

ONE ORDINARY AFTERNOON

ONE ORDINARY AFTERNOON – A.1 Do aliens really exist? Seite 19/23

a) True or false?

	Statement	True	False
1	Danny can talk to humans.	×	
2	Danny can talk to the strange astronauts.	×	
3	The Fire Chief talks to the aliens.		×
4	Sergeant Schmidt has a ray gun.		×
5	Danny is a cat.		×
6	There is a television crew at the scene.	×	

3. The Fire Chief can't talk to the astronauts. 4. The spaceman has a ray gun. 5. Danny is a dachshund.

b) What's going on at Oscar's house?
1. Oscar had known Danny for many years.
2. Details on object: The meteorite looked like a fist-sized piece of stone; it had travelled billions of miles across the galaxy; it created a cloud of steam which smelled good.
3. Danny is Oscar's dog and he can talk with humans and alien astronauts.
4. The visitors could not leave because they ran out of fuel.

ONE ORDINARY AFTERNOON – A.2 Not so ordinary after all ... Seite 20/24

The afternoon is not ordinary, because a meteorite hits Oscar's house. It is also not ordinary, because Danny, Oscar's dog, can talk to humans and to aliens.

ONE ORDINARY AFTERNOON – B.1 One ordinary past sentence Seite 20/24

a) 1b, 2d, 3e, 4c, 5a
b) The people came to see what happened. A meteorite **had crashed** into the house.
The firemen came after a neighbor **had called** them.
The astronauts explained they would repair Oscar's house. He **had asked** them about the damage.

ONE ORDINARY AFTERNOON – B.2 Oscar had known Danny for a long time Seite 21/25

had wanted / came / had travelled; were / had come; took place / had ended / had sealed

SUPERCHAMP, WHERE ARE YOU?

SUPERCHAMP, WHERE ARE YOU – A.1 Let's get it right! Seite 31/37

1. a) 2. d) 3. a) c) 4. c) d) 5. a) e)

Sebastian Beckmann, Bill Lowenburg, Carina Welsch · Englisch-Krimi 7/8 | 978-3-589-16754-8 | Illustration Lupe: shutterstock/Sonya illustration; Hintergrund: shutterstock/Tobias Steinert

SUPERCHAMP, WHERE ARE YOU – A.2 Who is who? Seite 31/37

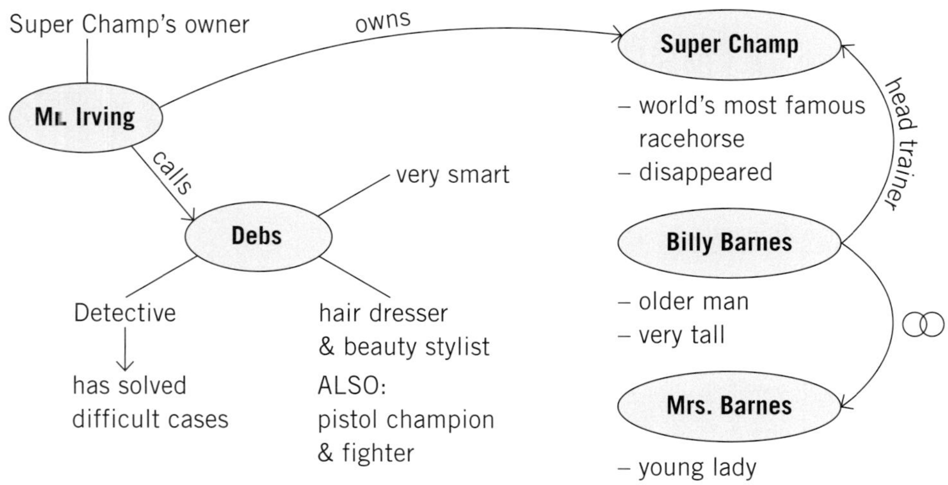

SUPERCHAMP, WHERE ARE YOU – A.3 The missing clue … Seite 32/38

He had been in the very next stall to his own; his blaze had been covered up with the same hair dye Mr. Barnes used to make himself appear younger for his wife.

SUPERCHAMP, WHERE ARE YOU – B.1 Go and find the evidence! Seite 32/38

a) Have a look.
   1. were called; 2. has been stolen; 3. had been covered;
b) Have another look.
   4. has been shown (line 5); 5. was shown (line 32);
   Advanced: z. B. were led (line 69); was introduced (line 64)
c) Think about it!
   Form of (to) be + -ed (regular verbs)/3. Spalte (irregular verbs) ▷ past participle (expert word)

SUPERCHAMP, WHERE ARE YOU – B.2 Let's be active and passive! Seite 33/39

a) Let's be passive!
   1. Detective Debs was called by Mr. Irving.
   2. The prize horse has been stolen by someone.
   3. Debs was introduced to Billy Barnes by him.
   4. The horses have been trained by Mr. Barnes for 25 years.
   5. Within days, SuperChamp would be recognized (by people).

b) Let's be active!
   1. Debs pulled the gag from Mrs. Barnes's mouth.
   2. Someone overturned furniture in a fight.
   3. Debs turned the lights back down.
   4. Many people did not take her seriously.
   5. A pretty young woman showed Detective Debs to the paddock.

TO GOOD TO BE TRUE

TO GOOD TO BE TRUE – A.1 Are you on the right track? Seite 47

1. False: 6 languages (line 3)
2. True (line 1)
3. False: she is very strong, international powerlifting champion, Womens's World Karate champion (line 11–13)
4. False: he is a financial advisor (line 35)
5. True (line 70)
6. True (line 81–82)
7. False: The white car was reported stolen, he and his friends charged of fraud and extortion, colleagues attacked Lisa and tried to kill her (line 110–112).

Sebastian Beckmann, Bill Lowenburg, Carina Welsch · Englisch-Krimi 7/8 | 978-3-589-16754-8 | Illustration Lupe: shutterstock/Sonya illustration; Hintergrund: shutterstock/Tobias Steinert

TO GOOD TO BE TRUE – A.2 Too good to be true? Seite 48

a) He took the exact opposite of the details in Buck's story and knew to go the opposite direction and that kidnappers often have their victims in abandoned warehouses
b) Everything seemed to be too easy and obvious, the witnesses all followed all the same story in every single detail, so he knew something must be wrong

TO GOOD TO BE TRUE – B.2 Easy peasy lemon squeezy! Seite 49

a) children b) UC c) pieces d) cars e) UC f) UC

TO GOOD TO BE TRUE – B.3 Go and find them! Seite 49

b. Too good to be true is a story about Johan Bopp, called Boppy, who runs a detective agency and who is able to speak six languages. One Thursday morning, a man came in, introduced himself as Tomas Buck explained that his wife had been kidnapped in front of his eyes. Boppy and his assistant Lisa could see that Buck had a dirty suit, a split lower lip and a small trickle of blood running from his nose. Buck explained that the police cannot be involved because then he would never see his wife again. Lisa said that the kidnappers chose his wife to get a lot of money because they had known he was rich.

c.

Countable		Uncountable
story	assistant	blood
agency	suit	police
languages	lip	money
Thursday morning	trickle	
man	nose	
wife	kidnapper	
eyes		

TO GOOD TO BE TRUE – B.4 Practice! Seite 50

Countable:	How many ...?;	These;	a lot of;	many;	a few
Uncountable:	How much ...?;	This;	a lot of;	much;	a little

TO GOOD TO BE TRUE – B.5 Let's take some action! Seite 50

1. many
2. a lot
3. much
4. Many/A lot of
5. little
6. many/a lot of +
7. A few
8. A lot of
9. much

THE GREAT PIZZA ROBBERIES

THE GREAT PIZZA ROBBERIES – A.1 What happened when? Seite 56/62

f, c, b, e, a, d

THE GREAT PIZZA ROBBERIES – A.2 A robbery? Seite 56/62

a) If they had taken the money, the police would have worked harder to find the thieves.
b) They stole the pizza on Thursday to make it to Friday to get paid.

Sebastian Beckmann, Bill Lowenburg, Carina Welsch · Englisch-Krimi 7/8 | 978-3-589-16754-8 | Illustration Lupe: shutterstock/Sonya illustration; Hintergrund: shutterstock/Tobias Steinert

THE GREAT PIZZA ROBBERIES – B.1 Off you go! Seite 57/63

Statements

1.	"They **are** *(to be)* welcome to stop by the shop for a slice of pizza." ***(simple present)***	→	He said that they **were** welcome to stop by the shop for a slice of pizza. ***(simple past)***
2.	"I'**m dealing** with *(to deal with)* bank robberies." ***(simple present progressive)***	→	Kratz said that he **was dealing** with bank robberies. ***(simple past progressive)***
3.	"A teenage boy **ran up** and **pointed** *(to run up/to point)* a pistol." ***(simple past)***	→	He said that a teenage boy **had run up** and **had pointed** a pistol. ***(past perfect)***
4.	"You **have discovered** (to discover) my secret." ***(present perfect)***	→	William said that he **had discovered** his secret. ***(past perfect)***
5.	"If only I **had known**." (to know) ***(past perfect)***	→	He said that if only he **had known**. ***(past perfect)***
6.	"I **am not going to waste** my time with a pizza!" (to waste) ***(going to-future)***	→	Kratz said that he **was not going to waste** his time for a pizza. ***(was/were + going to)***
7.	"**I'll have a look** (to have a look) into this myself and **I'll see** (to see) you on Friday." ***(will-future)***	→	He said that he **would have a look** into that himself and **he would see** him on Friday. ***(would/conditional)***

Questions

Questions with question words "*Why* **didn't** you **tell** me?"	→	Joe asked *why* William **hadn't told** him.
Yes/No Questions "There **is** a baby?"/"Is there a baby?"	→	Joe asked *if/whether* there **was** a baby.

THE GREAT PIZZA ROBBERIES – B.2 Track them down! Seite 58/64

1. line 24–25: *Joe said that he **understood**. If his officers **had** any spare time, they **were** welcome to stop by the shop for a free slice or two and he **could** update them.*
2. line 32–33: *Joe remarked that he couldn't understand. He said that none of the other delivery people **got robbed**, just him.*
3. line 34: *William replied that maybe it **was** because he **delivered** to the bad part of town.*
4. line 35: *Joe said that that **was** possible. He asked why the thief **didn't take** his money, too.*
5. line 36: *William answered that he **had** no explanation.*
6. line 54: *Joe asked what the meaning of that **was**.*
7. line 55: *William replied that Joe **had discovered** his secret.*
8. line 60: *William replied that he **was** ashamed and that he **wanted to work and earn** money, but he paid so little that some weeks they **couldn't make** it to Friday.*
9. line 67: *William's wife said that they **couldn't make** a fire there or they **would be discovered.***
10. line 70: *Joe asked why he **had faked** the robberies in fron of witnesses.*

THE GREAT PIZZA ROBBERIES – B.3 The other way around Seite 59/65

1. Kratz: "Am I supposed to get excited about a missing pizza?"
2. Joe: "I can't understand what's going on."
3. William: "I deliver to the bad part of town."
4. William: "You have discovered/discovered my secret."
5. William: "We can't make it to Friday."

Sebastian Beckmann, Bill Lowenburg, Carina Welsch · Englisch-Krimi 7/8 | 978-3-589-16754-8 | Illustration Lupe: shutterstock/Sonya illustration; Hintergrund: shutterstock/Tobias Steinert